Best Wishes

Ballyshannon Belcoo Bertincourt

The History of the 11th Bn. The Royal Inniskilling Fusiliers
(Donegal and Fermanagh Volunteers) in the First World War

by W. J. Canning

The voice of nature was not there, the birds and bees sang not;
The landscape's beauty blasted, with withering shell and shot.
The music was the roar of guns, the fragrance weeping smoke,
As the last half hour, the thunderous shower, the leaden volley broke.

One of the Eleventh
1st July 1916

Copyright © W. J. Canning 1996
All rights reserved

Published by W.J. Canning, Dunsilly Lodge, Antrim.

Printed by William Trimble Ltd., 8 & 10 East Bridge Street, Enniskillen.

ISBN 0 9528487 0 8

Contents

Chapter 1 - An Early Memory — page 1
Chapter 2 - The Ulster Volunteers in Donegal and Fermanagh — page 3
Chapter 3 - War is Declared — page 13
Chapter 4 - The Donegal Regiment — page 15
Chapter 5 - Changing Times — page 20
Chapter 6 - Enthusiasm and Inspections — page 22
Chapter 7 - Further Preparations — page 26
Chapter 8 - On to France — page 30
Chapter 9 - Infantry Weather — page 34
Chapter 10 - A New Beginning — page 37
Chapter 11 - Distinguished Conduct — page 41
Chapter 12 - An Unfortunate Accident — page 52
Chapter 13 - Dummy Trenches — page 55
Chapter 14 - Tunnelling, Digging and Shelling — page 58
Chapter 15 - The Somme — page 64
Chapter 16 - Distinguished Service — page 76
Chapter 17 - Knobkerries by Moonlight — page 79
Chapter 18 - At the Moon's Rise — page 84
Chapter 19 - Another Year — page 90
Chapter 20 - Battle of Messines — page 94
Chapter 21 - Passchendaele - Fighting in the Mud — page 107
Chapter 22 - Refitting and Training — page 116
Chapter 23 - Cambrai — page 118
Chapter 24 - The Unkept Promise — page 122
Chapter 25 - The System Still Works — page 125
Chapter 26 - Farewell to the Eleventh — page 127
Chapter 27 - "..And when the War is Over.." — page 130

Decorations Won by the Eleventh — page 141

Roll of Honour — page 144

Index — page 156

Thanks — page 170

Acknowledgments — page 172

CHAPTER 1
An Early Memory

I vividly recall as a boy at home near Burt in Donegal finding an old rifle and bayonet hidden in a chimney in our home. There was also an old bandolier and a slouch hat on the top of a wardrobe in another room and hanging on the wall a picture of a young man wearing the bandolier and holding a rifle at the slope.

In answer to my persistent boyish questioning my mother told me this was my uncle Samuel who had been an Ulster Volunteer. He died as a young man in 1919. He had been found medically unfit for military service and had not been subjected to the horrors of the trenches.

There was little discussion about all this in our home except that my father sometimes referred with great admiration to a school pal of his - Stewart Buchanan - who was killed at the Somme. According to my father he had always been a very daring fellow. My father also spoke highly of the Connaught Rangers and their gallant action throughout the war.

During my childhood several quiet determined men occasionally visited us at different times and I learned from the respectful attitude to them that they too had served in the Great War. I regret that no one recorded anything they may have said of their experiences. Perhaps they were very reticent about it all and content to let it fade into historical obscurity. They were country men of Donegal, used to the land and the soil, and they had been brought together with their counterparts from Fermanagh by a war many may not have understood and which had a profound impact on these rural communities. These men of the farms and villages of Donegal and Fermanagh became the 11th Battalion The Royal Inniskilling Fusiliers (Donegal and Fermanagh Volunteers). It is hoped that this record of men from this community will serve as a memory to them and of the Battalion in which they lived, fought and died. These men forged a proud place for themselves and their Regiment in that awful conflict.

This book is not written to glamorise the war but is an attempt to promote mutual understanding of the significance of events then and their consequences for the future.

Many years later I joined the Inniskillings and then I became truly aware of the honour of the Regiment and the great significance attached to these events. The formal teaching of Regimental History was an important part of a young soldier's training and the deeds of World War One were of particular pride.

This book owes much to these memories and it is important to remind oneself of the magnificent part played by men from all over Ireland in a war they found hard to comprehend. A war in which Irishmen of all creeds served and whose achievements added a splendid lustre to the name of Ireland throughout the world.

CHAPTER 2
The Ulster Volunteers in Donegal and Fermanagh

Every newspaper from about 1912 has many huge headlines in reaction to the Ulster Volunteers. Nearly every village and townland had some smattering of the Volunteer movement. The story starts in the months which preceded the outbreak of the War in Europe when Britain was dealing with a dangerous situation in Ireland.

Sir Edward Carson created the original Ulster Volunteer Force and it soon became known world-wide. His belief was that if Parliament were to impose its stated intention of forcing the Protestant people of Ulster into an Irish Parliament without their consent there would be a terrible civil war in the country. If resistance was not properly organised then the consequences would be chaotic and bloody. The fate of the Government was totally linked to its Home Rule Bill. Failure to carry it through meant defeat in the Commons as the Irish Nationalist party had the balance of power. Carson realised the only solution for his followers' political ideals meant convincing the people of Great Britain that the Protestants of Ulster would fight for all they prized so highly. In this belief he sanctioned the forming of the Ulster Volunteer Force, which became organised on a local basis.

When the War broke out there were over eighty thousand men between sixteen and sixty-five in its ranks. These men with such varying ages were organised together following the model of the Territorial Army. Part of their dress seemed to emulate the Boers. Also it is a remarkable coincidence that they trained in Finner Camp which was provided to train soldiers for the Boer War.

Many of these men were members of the Orange Order. The Order which dedicated itself to maintaining the Protestant tradition was well used to marching. Building on its memories of battle provided the ideal organisation from which a citizen army could be mustered.

So in the autumn of 1912 a series of meetings were held all over Ulster. Crowds in many towns were addressed by Carson. Men marched with wooden guns.

A "Solemn League and Covenant" was signed on 28th September which was named Ulster Day. Many men signed with their own blood and the women had a separate Declaration. Over four hundred and seventy-one thousand signatures were obtained. The Ulster Unionist Council was the controlling body and was led by Carson and Craig. The men who had been drilling with their wooden guns came under one command. The original Ulster Volunteer Force officially came into being in January 1913.

Large meetings of Unionists were held in South Fermanagh at Rosslea, Florencecourt, Letterbreen, Derrylin, Kinawley, Brookeborough, Greenhill, Maguiresbridge, Lisnaskea and Ballindara. These were all held in July 1912 and it was for the purpose of registration.

On 29th August 1912 there was a report which said that large numbers of men were drilling and had become expert shots with military rifles. It was calculated that about sixty thousand rounds of ammunition were used weekly at the ranges and the number of young men practising shooting had constantly grown in spite of the efforts of the government to delay the formation of the Unionist clubs.

Colonel Davidson D.S.O. and a JP lately commanding officer of the 27th Inniskillings had said that no one was bound to obey an unlawful order. People who asked what Loyalists would do should remember that there were farmers in Ulster who could do a good deal more than the Boers.

There was a gathering in Enniskillen on 18th September 1912 at which Sir Edward Carson MP, KC, and Sir Hugh Cecil MP were present and it was noted that there were to be no flags in this procession except the one, the Union flag. Men would march four abreast in the procession. Co. Fermanagh men would take first place and friends from neighbouring counties following in alphabetical order, being counties Cavan, Donegal and Monaghan. These were originally described as irregular infantry and here the effect of careful drill was well marked. The Lurg Infantry, composed of young men formed in companies from Irvinestown and the Kesh area numbering two hundred men under the command of Major D'Arcy Irvine, Rev. W. Stack and Mr. M. T. Stack marched with remarkable precision. The dressings and distances were well kept. The men carried themselves well and altogether they were an exceptionally fine lot of drilled men.

The interesting thing is that the Impartial Reporter said that there were no disturbances and that the Orangemen and Nationalists in these parts had an understanding between them not to interfere with each other's party adventures.

By then an enormous Ulster Volunteer Indemnity Fund had been established which stood at considerably over eight hundred thousand pounds. A full amount of a million sterling was assured by members of the provisional government executive.

In December 1913 the Fermanagh Volunteers were inspected by General Sir George Richardson which gave the force a stimulus in recruiting and esprit de corp. On his return from a further inspection in the course of a few months he found a larger and better disciplined force. Fermanagh had been behind its sister counties in the province in raising volunteers. For the short time the Fermanagh men had been drilling they showed excellent results and so pleased was General Richardson with the drilling that he sent an officer from headquarters to take up his residence in the county. The total number inspected by the General in the county was thirty officers and one thousand, eight hundred and twenty-seven other ranks. These were all men who had regularly attended the drills and no casuals were permitted in the ranks to swell the numbers. The following is the official list of the various companies inspected:-

1st Battalion: Castle Irvine six officers and three hundred and eighty-eight men; Clonelly five officers and two hundred and twelve men.

2nd Battalion: A total of seven officers and two hundred and seventy-nine men from the area Aghnadrum, Crom, Newtownbutler, Lisnaskea, Maguiresbridge and Kinawley.

3rd Battalion: Enniskillen, Florencecourt, Blaney, Lisbellaw, Tempo and Brookeborough: twelve officers and seven hundred and twenty-eight men.

Of the 3rd Battalion Enniskillen had produced three officers, Florencecourt two, Lisbellaw one, Tempo two, Brookeborough two.

Enniskillen had one hundred and seventy-eight men, Florencecourt ninety-nine, Blaney one hundred and ten, Lisbellaw one hundred and sixty-five, Tempo seventy men, Brookeborough one hundred and six men.

At a church service in Lisbellaw, where some two hundred and fifty members attended, the clergyman preaching the address said that he trusted that no one was present through feelings of pride or vain glory in their numbers. He trusted that no one was present with feelings of animosity towards those who differed from them in religion and politics. There was a noble spirit in the ranks of the Volunteers and the Protestants of Ulster to retain the invaluable blessings of their heritage. They wanted to be left alone to live in peace and do their daily work quietly. They had no desire to keep this liberty to themselves but the object of the struggle was for the welfare of the whole land.

After a number of consultations and meetings, it was finally decided that

County Fermanagh be divided into three Battalion areas, and that the men enrolled in the North portion of the county, including the villages of Ballinamallard, Irvinestown, Kesh, Pettigo, and Belleek should form the 1st Battalion Fermanagh Regiment U.V.F., and be under the command of Major C. C. D'Arcy Irvine of Castle Irvine, Irvinestown, and that those enrolled in the southern portion of the county, including the town of Maguiresbridge, Lisnaskea and Newtownbutler, etc., should form the 2nd Battalion Fermanagh Regiment U.V.F., under the command of the Earl of Lanesborough; and that those enrolled in the middle of the county including the town of Enniskillen, Lisbellaw, Tempo, Brookeborough, Derrygonnelly, should form the 3rd Battalion Fermanagh Regiment, U.V.F., under the command of Mr. Charles, F. Falls, with Mr. S. C. Clarke as adjutant.

These three Battalions formed the Fermanagh Regiment under the command of Viscount Crighton, D.S.O. Each man was provided with a cap, belt, haversack, puttees, bandolier, water bottle and rifle, and the officers wore an armlet distinguishing their rank, and all ranks wore a bronze badge with the Motto "For God and Ulster" with their regimental number inscribed. The men were trained by competent instructors appointed in each district. The 3rd Battalion had very suitable rifle ranges at Topped Mountain and Florencecourt and each man had to pass his musketry test and proficiency test in drill, etc., before he obtained the U.V.F. badge to be worn in his coat. All motor-cyclists were enrolled in a special corps Intelligence Branch known as Dispatch Riders and kept up communication over all Ulster. Fermanagh had a large number of these dispatch riders, who carried all orders and communications between the various Battalions and the head quarters of the force at Belfast.

The following is a copy of the 3rd Battalion Orders for the 13th April 1914 - Easter Monday:-

3rd BATTALION FERMANAGH REGIMENT U.V.F.

Battalion orders for Monday, 13th April, 1914 (Easter Monday), by C. F. Falls, Officer Commanding:-

The Battalion will assemble at 11.00 a.m. and form up in Quarter Column on the Cricket Ground, Broad Meadow, Enniskillen.

Company Commanders will be responsible for the attendance of their Companies at the hour named, but every effort will be made to secure sufficient train accommodation and reduced fares.
The Battalion will proceed to Derrygore for Company, Battalion, and

extended order drill, and will march back to Enniskillen in time to enable those travelling by rail to catch the 4.40 p.m. train.

All Volunteers should be quietly and neatly dressed and shall parade without arms, but wearing bandoliers, haversacks, water bottles, armlets and belts, and if possible puttees or gaiters. It is very desirable that Volunteers should wear a grey soft felt hat, which can be obtained in Enniskillen, as this would greatly improve the appearance of the Battalion on parade. Each man will bring his own rations for the day in his haversack.

Note:
No man will be allowed to leave the Ranks without the leave of his Company Commander, to be obtained through his Squad Leader. Every man must remember that he is a member of U.V.F. and obey his Officers' Orders in a smart and soldier-like way and conduct himself during the day in a sober, respectable and orderly manner so as to bring credit to the Battalion and the Force. Volunteers will remain under Military discipline until they are dismissed at their Drill Centres, and any man disobeying this order or conducting himself in a manner calculating to bring discredit on the Force will be struck off the roll of the U.V.F.

3rd Battalion, Fermanagh Regiment, U.V.F.
N.B. - Before using his water bottle each Volunteer should carefully and thoroughly cleanse same with boiling water.

Such was the discipline of the Battalion. On Friday the 12th June, 1914, the 3rd Battalion, Fermanagh Regiment, was inspected by Major General Sir George Richardson commanding the U.V.F., accompanied by Colonel Hackett-Payne, on the Enniskillen Horse drillfields at Castle Hume near Enniskillen. This inspection was a great success, at which over one thousand two hundred officers and other ranks, including seventy-one nurses, with the full complement of transport, were on parade and highly complimented by the Inspecting Officer. The following were the Officers of the Battalion:

THIRD BATTALION FERMANAGH REGIMENT U.V.F.
Officer Commanding - Charles F. Falls.
Second in Command - Captain Arthur Egerton, D.S.O.
Adjutant - S. C. Clarke.
Quartermaster - Cyril Falls.

Transport Officer - Herbert C. Gordon.

A Company (Lisbellaw)	Coy Commander	Robert Devers
B Company (Lisbellaw)	Coy Commander	John Dunlop
C Company (Tempo)	Coy Commander	Rev. J. O. Wilson
D Company (Cooneen)	Coy Commander	James Wilson
E Company (Brookeborough)	Coy Commander	Lieut. Col. Doran
F Company (Enniskillen)	Coy Commander	Charles Pierce
G Company (Enniskillen)	Coy Commander	George Evans
H Company (Florencecourt)	Coy Commander	Rev. J. F. Hewitt
I Company (Letterbreen)	Coy Commander	Robert McCourt
K Company (Beechmount)	Coy Commander	John Crawford

Early in 1914 the Fermanagh Volunteers attended a large camp for training at Knockballymore, near Clones in Co. Monaghan. At Knockballymore the site selected for the camp proved an almost ideal place for the purpose, as it was within convenient distance of Clones and while within the county of Fermanagh was on the very border of Monaghan, so it suited all counties equally well. A large house, extensive yard and spacious offices, which had been vacated for some years and were all generously placed at the disposal of the camp by the Earl of Erne, provided pleasant accommodation for officers and men and working staff.

The main house was utilised as Officers' quarters and the men were made very comfortable in the large and airy granaries and offices surrounding three sides of the courtyard. All arrangements and discipline were carried out on strict military lines. The membership of the camp was confined to Battalion staffs, company commanders, section and squad leaders and drill instructors of the three Fermanagh and the two Monaghan Battalions.

This gave the non-commissioned officers good practical training and fitted them to pass their skills on in several districts on their return home. Little did they realise how vital this preliminary training would be in the years that lay ahead.

There were over two hundred and fifty men in the camp. The messing took place in a very fine marquee erected in the yard in which all the men were able to dine together. A right jolly crowd they were when they sat down at the fifteen long tables, keen appetites whetted by the healthy exercise they went through on the parade ground and the surrounding hills. When the class was formed no visitors were permitted and no consideration whatever was given to intoxicating drink of any kind. This rule was strictly enforced.

Men were not allowed to leave the camp on any pretext unless they obtained a written permit to do so from the camp secretary. The main entries and boundaries were guarded during the day-time by camp police, specially detailed for the purpose, with armed guards on duty at night.

Great attention was paid to sanitation in the camp as it was on this that the health of all depended. No smoking was allowed in the sleeping quarters on account of the risk of fire. Badges were worn at all times. Camp police had orders to refuse admittance to all who were without a badge. All day long were the certain noise of marching feet, the words of command on the different parade grounds and many bugle calls plus other sounds familiar in a military barracks. The men came from widely separate districts, from Garrison, Belleek, Pettigo. Most of them were strangers to each other. From their arrival in camp they soon began to fraternise and in a short time the greatest good fellowship prevailed in all the ranks. It is interesting to note that when the camp started there had been numbers of police in the vicinity every day on the look-out for information. When the men went to church on Sunday they were carefully counted by two or three constables who had apparently been detailed for that purpose.

Lectures were given in a large mess tent in the evening by Major Madden, a former Officer of the Irish Guards who was the chief instructor. These were particularly definite, concise and couched in a language that made its meaning plain even to the dullest understanding. Both officers and men fully appreciated these lectures and most of them provided themselves with pencils and notebooks in which they made copious notes on important points.

Although the weather was not good it did not interfere with the work of the men. When heavy rain fell, their personal comfort was of secondary importance compared to gaining military proficiency. On several occasions the officers wanted to postpone training because of the rain but the men prevailed on them to allow the programme to continue. Night attacks were practiced, marksmanship improved and a further camp was planned for June.

It was noted also that the police had attempted to enter the camp and proceeded to where a squad of men were at musketry practice. They asked for their names and addresses but the men refused, referring them to the officer in charge. The sergeant then wanted to inspect the rifles but this was also peremptorily stopped by the officer on duty. The two policemen then left having gained little or no information about their visit. In fact a question in Parliament was asked about the conduct of the police on that occasion. During this time there was mutual respect between Unionists and Nationalists and they did not interfere in each other's activities.

County Donegal took a little longer to get organised. However the remarkable earnestness and enthusiasm that characterised the Volunteer movement in the southern districts of County Donegal, an extreme western outpost of Unionism in Ulster, was manifested in a practical and convincing manner at a splendid parade of the Ulster Volunteers on 4th March 1914. Six hundred officers and men of the 1st Battalion Donegal Regiment assembled at Rossnowlagh and were inspected by General Sir George Richardson. This particular Battalion, which was one of three in the county, had seven hundred and fifty men enrolled directly undergoing systematic drill and training. These were recruited from a very wide area of country extending from Ballyshannon to Ardara, a distance of some thirty-five miles.

These men were for the most part farmers' sons with a sprinkling of shopkeeping, business and professional classes. When it is remembered that they lived in predominantly Roman Catholic districts, it can be seen that it required considerably more courage and a very much stronger sense of duty on their part to make them come out into the open and proclaim publicly the side they were on, than was necessary in the case of their co-religionists who lived in the north eastern counties. The weather could not have proved more unfavourable for an outdoor fixture, the rain coming down in a heavy unceasing downpour the whole day.

Despite this fact the Battalion turned out in full strength and large numbers of spectators from the surrounding districts also braved the fury of the elements in order to be present and witness the inspection. The men numbered between six and seven hundred paraded on the fine strand which was firm underfoot, thus forming perhaps the very best site possible for the purpose. The men of the Battalion under the command of Mr. J. Sproule Myles JP of Ballyshannon wore haversacks, bandoliers and belts. They were a fine picture of well-setup, intelligent, determined young manhood. The Battalion was divided into eight companies which in turn were subdivided as follows:-

A Company	Ballyshannon, Rossnowlagh and Ballymagroarty under command of Charles Ross JP.
B Company	Ballintra and Hilltown under command of John Crawford.
C Company	Ballynakillen and Bigpark under command of James Johnston.
D Company	Laghey, Moyne and Culley under command of James Wray.
E Company	Donegal and Clara under command of Thomas Ervine.
F Company	Killynard under command of Thomas Ervine.
G Company	Inver under command of Joseph Kirk.
H Company	Killatee under command of George Henry.

The Inspecting Officer was accompanied by the Earl of Leitrim, commanding the Donegal Regiment and Mr. J. Sproule Myles JP. Colonel Hackett-Payne, Adjutant of the Ulster Volunteer Force, was unable to be present with the General as he had had an accident in Newtowncunningham.

A month later in April a very successful practice mobilisation of the whole Donegal Regiment took place. At midday mobilisation orders were issued for all men to be at their drill centres at eight that evening. Despite the size of the county and the scattered districts the company commanders had their orders within two hours.

Many companies had a full turnout by the required time. Many men were seen making their way from the fields and despite the great distances answered the roll call on time.

This was a considerable commitment given that in those days everyone worked a six day week and training on two evenings a week was pretty demanding.

As well as districts previously mentioned all Co. Donegal including Rathmelton, Letterkenny, Manorcunningham, Ray, Burt, Ballindrait, St. Johnston, Raphoe, Convoy, Ballylennon, Donoughmore, Castlefin took part in this exercise. In all there were four Battalions and all were at ninety-five per cent strength when they were dismissed that evening.

This was a considerable achievement given the short time since their formation and Lord Leitrim and his officers were well pleased.

After this a very large training camp was organised at Baronscourt the estate of the Duke of Abercorn. This encompassed every facet of training as well as having a field hospital supervised by Dr. Crosbie. Lord Leitrim was Camp Commandant and many prominent men of the time held positions of responsibility.

W.H. Wagentreiber was camp secretary. Among others present were Col Baillie of Raphoe Capt Moore and Major Pine-Coffin of Inishowen. Here the nine hundred men of Donegal and Derry City who were all specially selected benefited from the comprehensive training programme.

Around this time about six acres of Lord Leitrim's land at Firlaughan in Donegal which consisted of a covert for game had been deliberately set on fire. It was felt this was because of Lord Leitrim's political beliefs.

It is believed that the UVF in Donegal had actually obtained arms before the famous gun running to Larne. Lord Leitrim sent his driver Steve Bullock - later C.S.M. Bullock MC - to England with a lorry. Prior arrangements had been made. The rifles were concealed in barrels and driven by Bullock to Glasgow. The barrels were then consigned to a boat owned by his Lordship and taken by sea to Mulroy Bay. Here they were swiftly unloaded and the rifles speedily spirited away to the companies throughout Donegal.

CHAPTER 3
War is Declared

The whole Regiment continued training. They improved in all aspects of the military craft. It was a busy time of year for the farming community but this did not deter the men. There were practice turnouts and mobilisation exercises at Company level.

On 21st July 1914 a pair of Colours were ordered from Hobsons of London. Included in the device and inscription on one of them are the words "The Donegal Regiment". Hobsons still have the original tracing for the design of these colours. Unfortunately there is no record of who actually placed the order or how they were paid for. It is reasonable to assume however, that the Earl of Leitrim and other officers played a prominent part in this endeavour.

These were stirring times in Ulster as the original Ulster Volunteer Force continued to train and become better organised. It should be remembered that many of these men had already enlisted in the Regular Army. Lord Kitchener, the Secretary of State for War, said on the 7th August "I want the Ulster Volunteers". He was advised by Col. Hickman, President of the British League for the Defence of Ulster, to see Carson and Craig. Carson's position was not easy but he wanted to help. He had a severe responsibility towards the people of Ulster. He would be justly reproached by the people if all the fighting men of Ulster went to the war and in their absence the Home Rule Act was passed. The Act which in the first place they were formed to resist. Eventually - with much political and administrative detail in the background - the Ulster Division was formed. One important fact being that a fund had been set up which would help to equip the men.

As the men of Donegal and Fermanagh were involved in all this activity, two pistol shots fired in Sarajevo on June 28th 1914 resulted in the murder of the Archduke Francis Ferdinand and his wife. On 26th July Austro-Hungary declared war. The Russians mobilised four days later. Germany declared war on Russia - and a couple of days later - on France. On 2nd August Germany was refused free access through neutral Belgium and Britain was at the brink of war.

That weekend there was great activity in Ulster with speeches and demonstrations. On 4th August 1914 Britain declared war. Britain was not obligated - though many believed so - to go to war to defend neutral Belgium. However, the matter was of concern to her for practical and sentimental reasons. The British army started to mobilise and territorials and reserves were called up.

Concurrently recruitment for the Irish Volunteers had also been very successful, their aim being to support Home Rule. All of the north of Ireland had rapidly become a place bristling with arms. The situation was changing and becoming very dangerous. Redmond was only just able to get the Irish Party to agree and rename the Irish Volunteers the National Volunteers.

The question in the minds of many responsible people was just how long could these two bodies be kept under control?

On the one hand eager young Nationalists and on the other vigorous and determined young Loyalists. Both sides and their leaders were openly breaking the law and the police were very anxious.

CHAPTER 4

The Donegal Regiment

The Battalion was raised in September 1914 from the Donegal and Fermanagh Volunteers. Nearly all recorded information shows that The Donegal Regiment was the accepted title of the 11th Battalion. This demonstrates the territorial pride which existed in the county at the time. It surely also reflects the influence of Lord Leitrim and the respect in which he was held by the men of Donegal. The Battalion began training at Finner Camp in County Donegal on 20th September 1914 as part of 109 Brigade of the Ulster Division. They were mainly under canvas. This is in stark contrast to the official historian's record that when the German reserves were called up, hutted accommodation was already pre-positioned and even iced drinks were available.

Finner Camp was originally used to provide training facilities for soldiers during the Boer War and was known locally as the Boer War Camp. Progress was rapid since many of the men had undergone much elementary training and they were exceptionally keen. Already they were all benefiting from the Inniskilling tradition and memories were fresh of their deeds in South Africa.

One example of the thoroughness prevailing was, that regular equipment being scarce at that time, the men trained to march with their packs filled with steel bolts.

Writing home from Finner, Pte. Robert Roulston enclosed a photograph and said that this was the way the men dressed for training in the warm weather. The photo depicts the men in shirt sleeves. He also stated that the photo cost 3d which he said was a lot from a soldier's pay.

At the beginning of September the 11th Battalion was somewhat composite, the counties of Donegal and Fermanagh having contributed one company each and the third being formed by the British League for the support of Ulster. The Inniskillings were playing a prominent part in the Ulster Division which would be in the new Army.

The 11th Battalion was most fortunate in securing Lt. Col. William Hessey as their Commanding Officer. To date his career had been an enviable one and was familiar to all those who had served in the old 27th. Prior to taking over command of the 11th Battalion he had been in the reserve of officers of the Inniskillings and had reported to Omagh Depot at the outbreak of the war. His service with the

Regiment dated from 1890. He was Adjutant of the 1st Battalion in South Africa and served there from 1899 - 1902.

He was at the relief of Ladysmith. He was badly wounded at Colenso but this did not prevent him from taking part in the action at Vaal Krantz and Tugela Heights. He was present at the final triumph of the old 27th at Inniskilling Hill where their gallantry largely unlocked the way into Ladysmith.

Lt. Col. Hessey took part in the operations in the Transvaal and the actions at Belfast and Lydenberg. In South Africa he gained the reputation as the "Handyman" of the Inniskillings. This was because he took command of the Inniskillings at Ladysmith till the arrival of Major MacKenzie when he then became Adjutant and subsequently Quartermaster. He then was awarded a brevet majority and mentioned in despatches. He had the Queen's Medal with five clasps and the King's Medal with two clasps.

Later he was Adjutant of Durham University OTC from 1908 - 1912. He had an MA from Durham University and had retired in 1913 with the rank of Major. He became Temporary Lt. Col. on assuming command of the 11th Battalion on 27th October 1914.

Major the Earl of Leitrim became second in command of the 11th Battalion on appointment of Lt. Col. Hessey. It was a natural consequence in view of the untiring service he had given in the interests of the Ulster Volunteers. He was also Mess President of the Officers' Mess.

He had been an officer in the 9th Lancers and had served with the Imperial Yeomanry in South Africa. He was a prisoner along with Winston Churchill and they both escaped.

Major the Earl of Leitrim had been Commanding Officer of the Battalion during its formation and transition from the Ulster Volunteer Force and subsequently at Finner in September and October 1914.

An Officer Capt. R. L. Moore, who was well known locally, was appointed adjutant. Capt. Moore had previously served in the 3rd Hussars.

The Eleventh organised their first concert on Tuesday October 6th in a large marquee in the camp. The concert was directed by R.S.M. Bleakley. Great credit was given to the R.S.M. for bringing together such a fine musical entertainment in such a short time as he had only joined the Battalion a few days previously. The marquee was crowded with over four hundred men. Before the concert began humourous songs were sung by the audience, the hearty choruses filling the air.

The officers who had won the hearts of all the men were seated at eight o'clock. The officers were doing all they could for the welfare of these young Inniskillings.

Many songs and recitations were given. Lt. C. B. Falls recited "How we beat the favourite" and H. Carrothers song "Hulligan's Mule" were loudly encored.

Next day, Wednesday October 7th the Eleventh played their first football match. A and D Coys versus B and C Coys. B and C Coys won 3-1 after a very exciting game.

Pte. James Quigley from St. Johnston wrote home to his grandmother on 15th October and said that the weather was very frosty. Inside the tent at night appeared to be comfortable enough but it was bitterly cold on parade in the mornings.

In mid October a course in weapons training started. Twenty-five rounds had been allotted per man and only sixteen rifles for the Battalion so results were a little slower than usual.

Planning was also in hand to provide huts at Shane's Castle in County Antrim. At this early stage there was no indication of when they would be ready.

Route marches were continuing three times a week. It must be borne in mind that not all the men had as yet received a full issue of kit. All of them appeared to have been issued with boots thus making the route marches possible.

The Fermanagh company intended to have a march through their county for recruiting purposes as soon as they were issued with uniforms. The Battalion band would accompany them, LOL 624 Enniskillen having kindly loaned them their instruments.

The Battalion was working very hard in the best Inniskilling tradition to get itself up to the required standard and everyone was in good spirits.

Those who had enlisted for adventure and excitement would have found the attractions of Ballyshannon and Bundoran limited. The kindness of many local people helped to make the men's free time more tolerable.

Canon Naylor aided by these generous subscribers had made available in

Bundoran two large rooms for reading, writing letters and other activities. They could accommodate about seven hundred men. In Ballyshannon the men had the use of the Freemasons' Hall and billiard room.

The soldiers were highly regarded in the area. In November the magistrates had refused an application of district Inspector Hildebrand to close all public houses at eight o'clock in the evening. He believed if the order were made it would be for the good of the Empire and the town as well as the men! There were upwards of four thousand men in the camp.

Mr. Maguire, a local solicitor who appeared for the publicans, stated that everyone living in Ballyshannon or Bundoran knew there was no need for such an order. He had lived there for fifteen years when Finner Camp was first established. Many bodies of troops had been there but he had never known a more orderly or sober body of troops than these. Several publicans supported this and said that they had all observed the request by the military authorities not to serve drink to soldiers after 8.30 in the evening. The magistrates further remarked there had been no disturbances worth noting, neither had there been an increase in drunkenness in either town.

It was agreed drink would not be served to the soldiers after 8.00 p.m. and that licensed premises remain open as usual. Colonel Fegan - Commander of Lough Swilly Defences - had already ordered that men in uniform only be permitted in Enniskillen licensed premises from six to eight in the evening.

In mid November Lt. Douglas E. Crosbie RAMC was posted to the 11th Battalion as their first Medical Officer. A keen sportsman and superb organiser he was to become a popular and invaluable member of the Battalion.

At the 14th November 1914, the official strength of the Ulster division was thirteen thousand, two hundred and twenty-three officers and men. On that day the 11th Battalion was a total strength of seven hundred and three officers and men.

On November 20th - owing to the severity of the weather at Finner - six hundred and fifty men of the 11th Battalion marched in to Enniskillen. They occupied part of the Royal Barracks and Castle Barracks. Later in the month B Company arrived in Enniskillen by special train from Ballyshannon. They were quartered in the Industrial Hall. Mr. Reid A.S.C. had made every arrangement for the reception of the men who numbered two hundred and forty. This hall was heated by steam and the spacious ground floor held the dining table. The men slept in the large gallery which ran round the inside of the building. The Company Commander

Captain Sproule Myles was not with the company as he had been appointed to look after the brigade transport arrangements prior to the move to Randalstown. Again there was public comment on the fine stature of the men. One company was left at Finner to finish the musketry course. The companies rotated between Enniskillen and Finner until every company had completed the course.

This move stopped the Battalion from exposure in the severe weather and helped to reduce illness to a minimum.

Nov. 1914 ~ List of Officers 11th Battalion (Donegal Regiment)

Lieut-Col.	Hessey, W.F.
Major	The Earl of Leitrim
Captains	Falls, C.F., Myles J.S.
Adjutant	Moore, Capt. R.L.
2nd Lieuts.	McIntyre, L.W.; Moore, W.; Gordon H.C.; Butler, H.C.; Boyton, J.G.; Ballintine, J; Hart A.C.; Munn, E.M.; Wagentreiber, W.H.; Falls, C.B.; McCorkell, B.F.; Williamson, W.R.; Gilliland, G.F.; Craig, J.A.T.; McIldowie, J.D.

Included in the above list of officers was W. Moore who had been a Colour Sergeant before the War and had served mainly in China. He quickly became Company Sergeant Major in the Eleventh. He was commissioned in November 1914 and eventually became Adjutant. He was awarded the M.C. for his constant bravery and devotion to duty. His name appears regularly in the record as Adjutant and his thoroughness is reflected in all the written Battalion Orders. He died in Belfast in 1945 at the age of 74.

Joe Wallace from Carnamaddy near Burt had returned from Scotland as a boy. He was well used to the hard work of farming and to the open air. He recalled that he did not find Finner as bleak as some of the lads from Belfast. He remembered along with other men who were used to the land that the fellows from the cities and towns took a while to get used to the wildness of the place.

The Battalion at this stage was not yet wearing the Inniskilling cap badge but wore the Red Hand of Ulster badge on a metal background. It was called the "Dixie".

As the year drew to a close the men continued to work hard. Arrangements were made to release as many as possible for Christmas leave. A very workable arrangement provided for this and at the same time enabled essential duties to be undertaken by the minimum number required to fulfil them.

CHAPTER 5

Changing Times

In early January the Battalion marched to the hutted camp at Shane's Castle near Randalstown. The whole Brigade took part in this march complete with transport and field kitchens. At the end of each day tents were pitched and the soldiers slept where they had halted. There were no tent bottoms and the men slept in their blankets on the ground.

The Eleventh had first to march to Omagh to meet up with the other three Battalions from Finner. Their huts had been long awaited and meant the men were housed in less overcrowded conditions. Men were working day and night to finish the construction of the huts.

The weather was still severe and all the ground surrounding the huts became knee deep in mud. Everyone took great care not to slip off the duck boards which provided the walkways between the huts. B Coy was housed in Ridge Camp No. 3. Overall the living conditions for the men were greatly improved.

Life in the Eleventh was now changing quite significantly as it continued training and became more professional in every aspect of military necessity.

A course of battle practice and physical training was attended in Belfast by Sergeants T. Elliot, T. Williamson and G. Olphert. Recruiting was also going on and the Earl of Leitrim, Capt. R. L. Moore, Sgt. E. McConkey and Corporal J. Roulston were prominent in that activity and with some success.

Training of junior NCO's was also given a high priority and twelve men were promoted to Lance Corporal in early January to participate in this.

Early in February thirty-seven Ulstermen who had worked in Newcastle upon Tyne came in a draft. The Earl of Leitrim returned from recruiting duty and assumed command for a short while during the absence of Lt. Col. Hessey.

Various courses continued at a rapid pace and second Lt. L. Munn and Sergeant J. Hamilton were sent to the School of Instruction at Chelsea Barracks. Lt. H. Gallaugher was transferred from a P.T. course to a transport course. This illustrated the requirement for a capable officer to be trained in the transport techniques developing in the modern army.

The physique of the men has already been referred to several times. Sergeant J. Bryan Stewart was an Enniskillen man. He must have held the army record for great stature. He was six feet one and a half inches in height, chest forty-five inches and weighed twenty-four stone. He was an international water polo player and a rugby player as well as being a keen motorist. He was an old Portora boy and was eventually commissioned and served with the 16th Irish Division.

The following promotion appeared in the London Gazette. Temporary Second Lieutenants to be Temporary Lieutenants, G. M. Forde, B. F. McCorkell, E. M. Munn, R. G. Orr, G. H. Webb.

Further illustrating the developments within the Eleventh were the promotions to Company Sergeant Major of the following:

Sgt. R. McConley	B Coy	12th February 1915
Sgt. W. Iliffe	C Coy	16th February 1915
C/Sgt. Smart	D Coy	undated

Tragically Pte. Thomas Rowe was accidentally drowned in Belfast. His funeral was from the Mater Hospital. Lt. C. B. Falls, Major W. Fitzgerald and Capt. G. R. Irwin were present at the funeral. The firing party was provided by the Victoria Barracks' staff commanded by Sgt. Elliot. The coffin, which was draped with a Union Jack, was borne on a military gun carriage, on which were laid two beautiful wreaths from the officers and men of the deceased's Battalion. A military band was in attendance, and played an appropriate funeral march.

On 29th March a number of officers and NCO's went to Dollymount Camp, Dublin for various courses of instruction.

The Deputy Director of Medical Services in Ireland inspected the Battalion in the morning of 31st March. He also was very impressed with their fitness.

CHAPTER 6

Enthusiasm and Inspections

Training continued at a cracking pace. The roads all around County Antrim were echoing to the marching feet of the young soldiers. The weather started to improve. This was fortunate as there was one brigade route march each week and a Battalion route march a week for good measure.

The group spirit of the Battalion was now well developed. Religious feeling inspired the men in those days of training and remained with them in the days of war. The official historian noted that the General commanding the Division in France, to which they were attached on arrival for instruction, spoke of his amazement at finding so many Ulster men reading their Bible.

The Battalion took part in the magnificent Divisional Parade at Belfast on Saturday May 8th. Twenty seven officers and nine hundred and ninety one men were present.

Lt. Falls and a number of NCO's attended a Railway Transport course in Dublin in the middle of May.

At the seventh rifle course at the Irish Command School of Musketry Lt. J. Ballintine and Sgt. McCourt qualified as first class instructors along with Cpls. Williamson and Whittle. On the machine-gun course Lt. J. Hart showed great ability.

Other forms of training continued as well. Bayonet practice took up a lot of time and energy. Stripped to the waist when the weather permitted the soldiers charged at the dummies with great enthusiasm. Learning to parry an opposing comrade's bayonet was a slight foretaste of the nature of an encounter with the enemy.

The Battalion was in very good form. This was further demonstrated following an inspection by General Friend commanding the forces in Ireland when he expressed himself well pleased at their fitness and bearing.

For the first week of May Lt. Col. Hessey took over command of 109 Brigade when Brigadier T. E. Hickman C.B.E., D.S.O. was on leave. This is an extract from the report of the Superintendent of Gymnasia who also inspected the Battalion:

"The physical training of this Battalion is very good - the exercises being performed in good style. The men moved with great precision and were all keenly interested in their work".

In Randalstown and the surrounding area the soldiers were very welcome. Local facilities including the reading room and church halls were made available to them.

As well as the tight training programme other necessities of army life had to be completed including inoculations. Week-end leave was a most welcome respite. James Quigley looked forward to returning to the historic city of St. Johnston as he wryly put it in his letter home.

At Ridge Camp in Randalstown morale was very good and the Eleventh were in high spirits. This is aptly illustrated by this proclamation devised by the wags of the Eleventh. The address is to a soldier of some distinction CQMS McCullough.

He had enlisted originally in February 1891 and served in India, China and Singapore. He was mentioned in special General Orders and received the Tirah medal.

Then he served in South Africa and Egypt and had South African medal with six clasps. He re-enlisted in the Eleventh in September 1914 and was wounded at the Somme. He had eleven wounds and was hospitalised up to February 1917.

Including his previous service he was wounded a total of seventeen times. He was discharged in February 1919 having been a specialist instructor on the Lewis gun at Fermoy.

On the 4th of June a draft of sixty men joined from the Reserve Battalion. They too had to be inducted and trained at Randalstown.

The Viceroy Lord Wimborne accompanied by Lady Wimborne reviewed the whole brigade in the Deerpark at Shane's Castle.

Following the strenuous training of the past six months, Waterloo Day came as a well deserved and pleasant relief. This was celebrated by a brigade sports day. In those days it should be remembered that there were four Battalions to a Brigade. They all entered with great enthusiasm.

The President of the Sports Committee was Brigadier T. E. Hickman C.B.E.

FREEDOM OF RIDGE CITY

We the Lord Mayor, Aldermen & Citizens of the Loyal & Ancient Borough of Ridge City have much pleasure in presenting Com. Qrmsgt. Mc Cullogh 11th Innis Fus with the Freedom of the City for his courtesy, kindness & thoughtfullness in paying us this remote visit, we know that during the present European Crisis his duties are numerous, principally in Shell making & building up the future Generations. we know that his time is short with us & we pray that on some future occasion he will endeavour to cast his thoughts towards the Corps to which he first commenced his career, we have heard with delight that he is to succeed Kitchener at the War Office & we know that he will do honour to the name of Mc Cullough.

Signed on behalf of the Aldermen & Citizens this 25th Day of May 1915.

The proclamation for C.Q.M.S. McCullough

D.S.O. The Chairman was Lt. D. E. Crosbie RAMC. Major, the Earl of Leitrim and Lt. W. Knight of the Eleventh made up a hard working committee. In the scheduled time all the organisation was completed.

From far and near the friends of everyone flocked to see the fun. They were warmly welcomed and hospitably entertained. The weather was ideal and the course in Shane's Park was at its best and loveliest. The interest and rivalry between the Battalions produced such enormous entries. The whole morning was spent running off the various heats leaving the finals for the afternoon.

One of the many features of the day was an officers' race bare backed on mules. This resulted in many spills and an exciting finish was well won by Lt. Gallaugher of the Eleventh. Capt. Sewell was second. The men of the Eleventh featured prominently in the day's events. Pte. Arkless won the obstacle race. The officers relay race was won by the Eleventh. The Eleventh team won the wrestling on horseback.

Brigadier Hickman received a rousing cheer when he presented the prizes testifying to the pride of the men serving under such a distinguished soldier.

A glorious day came to an end with the massed bands playing and the crowd singing the National Anthem.

CHAPTER 7

Further Preparations

Drafts continued to arrive with the Eleventh and about forty men were transferred to the 12th (Reserve) Battalion at Finner Camp. Among those transferred at this time was R.Q.M.S. J. Bleakley.

On the evening of Wednesday 7th of July the Eleventh left Dublin via the North Wall. In fact they were the last major unit of the 36th (Ulster) Division to embark. There was an air of great excitement as they went on board. For the majority of them this was the first time they had been on a ship and certainly the first time they had left Ireland.

Mr. W. Trimble was present and this is part of his report.

At ___ p.m. the men fell in to march through the underground passage to join the four great transport vessels awaiting them. Through the courtesy of Lieut. H. C. Gordon - (who was busy looking after his men with fatherly care) - the writer was permitted on the transport, and it was a pleasure to see the men march on board in an orderly manner, conducting themselves like true gentlemen. There was no rowdiness, no yelling or shouting; all was in keeping with the good name the Division had earned. First trooped on board the Fermanagh men, then some of the Tyrones, and last came some of the Armagh and the Antrim men; also some of the Donegal men with Capt. Boyton. Out of about 800 only a few had indulged too freely considering the occasion and circumstances! The stewards on the boat were surprised at the soldierly bearing of the men, and said that no finer troops had ever crossed the channel.

As I said 'Good-bye, for the last time' to one Enniskillen lad, he retorted 'not for the last time, we mean to come home again.' I saw his meaning and replied, 'Au revoir, then'. 'That's better' he said as he warmly shook my hand.

The great ship cast her moorings and began to move gently from her berth. I called for a chorus from the boys in the stern just to cheer them a bit, and they sang with gusto 'Fare thee well, Enniskillen.'

The extreme kindness of a well known Ulsterman living in Dublin was widely reported. Mr. David Turner, his wife, and a number of their friends distributed cigarettes, matches, postcards and stamps to the men of the Eleventh.

A souvenir of the good will of their Dublin friends was sent aboard for the officers plus a large hamper for the N.C.O.'s.

Before the troopship sailed Major Lord Leitrim, accompanied by Major Falls and Major Moore came to the gangway. They expressed their gratitude to Mr. Turner and his assistants for the hospitable manner in which they had welcomed the troops and for their generous send off. So the Eleventh moved to Seaford, a town on the Sussex coast.

They were well received on arrival. England was new to the men and they made a good impression. They were very kindly treated and their behaviour was excellent which reassured the local residents who had been a little dismayed by the arrival of 'wild Irishmen'.

On the 15th of July, the Eleventh were inspected at Seaford by Lt. Gen. Sir A. G. Murray K.C.B. K.C.M.G. C.V.O. D.S.O. Deputy Chief of the Imperial General Staff and Colonel of the Regiment.

The Eleventh were well prepared and their distinguished Colonel voiced his appreciation of their efforts.

Training continued but at that stage there was still a shortage of Lee Enfield rifles. All other training went on in the pleasant surroundings and the men really liked the area. They were resolved to do their best and the group spirit continued to develop.

The London Gazette showed that H. Gallaugher and C. B. Falls became Temporary Lieutenants.

In Lt. Falls the Eleventh Battalion had as a junior officer, a man who was to distinguish himself very quickly as a military historian. He subsequently was a member of the Historical Section of the Committee of Imperial Defence writing many works including "The History of the Ulster Division". All of these being recorded in superb detail.

His father Sir Charles Fausset Falls who was a remarkable man enlisted in the Eleventh at the age of 54.

2nd Lt. J.R.M. Hanna was posted to B. Coy and 2nd Lts. J. A. Reid and T.

McCrea to C. Coy.

Interestingly the record shows that six men passed an examination for an appointment as shoeing smiths. It is unclear, however, if in fact they were trained to shoe horses or whether they were really cobblers as would befit an Infantry Battalion.

Another inspection followed on the 27th July by Field Marshal Lord Kitchener K.P. He was delighted with the appearance of all on parade. He congratulated the G.O.C. on the steadiness of the men and on their drill. He also commented he was glad to see a division so far advanced and ready for the front.

Later he said to Sir Edward Carson, doubtless referring to the New Armies only "Your Division of Ulstermen is the finest I have yet seen."

Lack of accommodation meant that it was a few weeks before the Eleventh could move to an area to fire its rifle course.

At the beginning of September it was at Bramshott and here the course was fired.

Sufficient rifles had now been issued as a result of Kitchener's visit. Unfortunately American ammunition appeared to give unsatisfactory results. Lt. Falls recalled that one soldier in the Eleventh missed the target twice at 600 yards. Previously on an Ulster Volunteer range he had seen the same man put five large bullets from an Italian Veterli into the bull's eye.

On 30th September the King inspected the Division. It was organised so that the march past of Artillery and Infantry was as short as possible. The King always insisted on waiting till the last man had gone by. It was a high test, splendidly executed and a masterpiece of staff work and drill.

This year of preparation for war was over and the Eleventh proudly shared in the following message sent by the King:

Officers, non-commissioned officers, and men, you are about to join your comrades at the front in bringing to a successful end this relentless war of over twelve month's duration.

Your prompt patriotic answer to the nation's call to arms will never be forgotten. The keen exertions of all ranks during the period of training have brought you to a state of efficiency not unworthy of my regular army.

I am confident that in the field you will nobly uphold the traditions of the fine regiments whose names you bear. Ever since your enrolment I have closely watched the growth and steady progress of all units. I shall continue to follow with interest the fortunes of your Division.

In bidding you farewell, I pray God may bless you in all your undertakings.

George, R. I.

CHAPTER 8

On to France

The Battalion had assembled at Bramshott Camp, Liphook in Surrey. Here all the vital but necessary work of administration and organisation had to be accomplished in a short time. It was a matter of checking and re-checking every detail. This is something most soldiers naturally detest. They don't take easily to mundane matters of administration. Already they had been through more than enough of it prior to leaving Ireland and they were impatient to be getting on with the main task of fighting. Those who have been involved with the movement of a large number of soldiers will be familiar with all the painstaking detail and hard work involved. Nominal rolls, kit checks, allocation of accommodation, feeding and medical arrangements to name but a few.

On 4th October the Advance Party left Bramshott at seven o'clock that morning. There were three officers and one hundred and nine men. The party included the machine-gun and transport section travelling to Southampton and thence to Le Havre and Cardonette.

On the evening of 5th October the main body of the Battalion left Liphook in two trains. There were twenty-seven officers and eight hundred and eighty-nine men. At Folkstone they embarked on the St. Oriel transport vessel and arrived at Boulougne at 3 o'clock in the morning and marched to Ostrohove rest camp. They remained there all day following their early morning march.

The next day the Battalion moved by train - some of the train was horse boxes - to Flesselles and then marched to Cardonette arriving in the evening. This is where they met the Advance Party again and billeting arrangements had been organised following the long march. There was some confusion trying to find billets in the dark.

General Sir C. C. Monro KCB who commanded the 3rd Army inspected the Battalion on 9th October and complimented them on their smart turnout and fine physique.

All the next week was taken up by training and normal duties. However a foretaste of things to come was experienced when the Battalion had gas training by the Chemical Advisor of 3rd Army. The Battalion wore their gas helmets and gas was released to test them.

The morale of everyone was very high and the Donegal and Fermanagh men began to get acquainted with the rural area and compare it with the farms and fields they had left behind. In some cases the French tried to sell apples to the soldiers.

On 21st October the Battalion marched out of Cardonette at eight o'clock. They marched to an assembly area east of Flesselles where they met up with the other Battalions of the Brigade. The whole Brigade was ordered to march across country northwards in artillery formation to Namour. After this exhausting march the Battalion continued to Condas. It arrived dirty and weary at ten o'clock that night and bedded down in straw on the floor.

Following those days in this location the Battalion moved on the morning of the 25th to Pouchevillers. This journey lasted over sixteen hours and a tired but cheerful body of men slept in billets that night.

The next day the Battalion was marching again - this time to Hedauville. Arriving at noon the men were allocated their living quarters under canvas stirring afresh memories of Finner. The aim here was to instruct everyone in the art of living, working and fighting in the trenches. During this time the Battalion was attached to the 11th Infantry Brigade of the 4th Division.

The last few days of October saw the Companies of the Eleventh dispersed among other units for training. A and B Companies went into the trenches for three days. A Coy was attached to the Rifle Brigade's 1st Battalion and B Coy got to know their counterparts in the Royal Hampshires, mainly countrymen like themselves. Here they had their first casualty - Pte. Montgomery slightly wounded in the knee. This was in the line of trenches north of Hamel. The remainder of the Battalion was under instruction in camp. Then C and D Companies went into the trenches and A and B Companies returned to camp.

This letter gives an impression of a soldier's life in those early days.

From 11th Battalion

Tuesday, 19th October, 1915

Dear J____, Just a line to say I have arrived safe in France, and I am enjoying myself, and am in the best of health and spirits. This is a lovely country and the French people are all very obliging and kind to us. We get it very hard to understand the language, and it is the same with them, but we manage to get on all right with them.

We have no need to grumble at all. We are billeted in a small village and have everything we require. The only thing we did miss was the old Woodbine cigarettes when we came here first; but we have got some from across the channel since, for you know there was no earthly chance of getting Woodbines out here.

I saw the *Impartial* this last two weeks. It was some of the boys got it from home and I was glad to get a read at the old paper. I told J____ to give you my address so as you can drop me a paper every week.

You can drop me an *Impartial* and an odd line, it will always be some news from the old town. Well J____ I have no strange news nor no complaints, but be sure and write soon and tell me all the news. Remember me to all at home, and also the old staff. I will close with best regards from your old chum,

J. R. Irvine

At the end of October there were thirty officers and nine hundred and ninety-eight other ranks of the 11th Battalion in France.

This is the nominal roll of officers signed by Lord Leitrim:

Appendix 1
11th (S) Battalion Royal Inniskilling Fusiliers
Nominal Roll of Officers who came out with the Battalion

RANK	SURNAME	CHRISTIAN NAME IN FULL	DATE OF EMBARKATION	REMARKS
Lieut Col.	Hessey	William Francis	5.10.15	
Major	Leitrim	The Earl of	4.10.15	
Major	Falls	Charles Fausset	5.10.15	
Captain	Sewell	William Tait	5.15.15	
Captain	Myles	James Sproule	5.10.15	
Captain & Adjt.	Moore	William	5.10.15	
Captain	Butler	Henry Cavendish	5.10.15	
Captain	Boyton	James Godfrey	5.10.15	
Captain	Ballintine	Joseph	5.10.15	
Captain	Forde	Gordon Miller	5.10.15	
Lieut.	Wagentreiber	William Harnett	5.10.15	
Lieut.	Gordon	Herbert Crawford	5.10.15	
Lieut.	McCorkell	Barry Francis	5.10.15	
Lieut.	Orr	Robert Gerald	5.10.15	
Lieut.	Webb	George Henry	5.10.15	
Lieut.	Gallaugher	Henry	4.10.15	

Lieut.	Falls	Cyril Bentham	5.10.15
Lieut.	Irvine	Gerard Mervyn Frederick	4.10.15
2nd Lieut.	Craig	John Arnott Taylor	5.10.15
2nd Lieut.	M'Ildowie	John Durie	5.10.15
2nd Lieut.	Hart	Andrew Chichester	5.10.15
2nd Lieut.	Williamson	William Robert	5.10.15
2nd Lieut.	Munn	Lionel Oulton Moore	5.10.15
2nd Lieut.	Knight	William Madden	5.10.15
2nd Lieut.	Grant	Robert	5.10.15
2nd Lieut.	Rutledge	Laurence Hugh Nesbit	5.10.15
2nd Lieut.	Browne	Andrew Douglas Comyn	5.10.15
2nd Lieut.	Hanna	John Riddell Musgrove	5.10.15
Lieut.	Crosbie	Douglas Edward	5.10.15 Medical Officer
Lieut. & Quartermaster	Firth	James Webster	5.10.15

LEITRIM, Major,
Comdg. 11th (S) Battalion Royal Inniskilling Fusiliers

CHAPTER 9

Infantry Weather

It has to be remembered that as the Donegal and Fermanagh men were getting used to their new way of life a great deal had happened since August 1914. The terrible and exhausting retreat from Mons had taken place. The battle of the Marne was meant to be the turning point of the war ensuring the enemy's loss of speed and mobility. The Germans realised the defensive potential of the heights above the Aisne.

The static warfare which ensued was a foretaste of things to come. The Battle of the Aisne was almost a rehearsal for the trench warfare for which the 11th Inniskillings were now preparing. It was not the anticipated mobile warfare for which they had joined the Colours.

There was another side to it as well. The trenches became a way of life - a society of its own. It acquired its own dynamics and identity. It became a society encapsulating every activity. More men were engaged in logistical organisation than fighting. Rearwards from the trenches stretched a vast organisation of supply dumps, training areas, hospitals, repair shops, evacuation systems and burial squads to name a few.

The weather in the first week of November was very bad. Heavy rain fell all day and everyone and everywhere was saturated.

On 3rd November the Battalion marched out of Hedauville in the morning and arrived at Candas in the late afternoon. The rain was very heavy and their great coats were wet through. The nightmare of every soldier and Quartermaster occurred on this march. The men's boots were found to be in a very bad condition. Five men fell out in the march - two from sprained ankles caused by bad boots.

The remainder of the week was spent in routine duties and training. A detachment of five officers and fifty men was sent off to Brigade Headquarters for instruction in Bombing on 6th November.

The next week was very cold with a keen frost and several falls of snow. In these conditions the routine work of improving billets continued in conjunction with all the other activities of moving stores, ammunition and rations. During 20th and 21st November the Battalion was inoculated. It was still freezing and very cold. At 8.30 on 27th November the Battalion left Candas and marched to Brucamps. This was a bracing march in very hard frost and the Battalion arrived in very good order in the early afternoon. In the second week of December the billets were inspected by the Divisional Commander. The Battalion received praise for the high standard of the billets and the excellent sanitary arrangements of the whole village. Earlier training in Ulster in these important elements had paid off.

This letter from J.R. Irvine of Enniskillen aptly sums up the reaction of the soldiers to their introduction to the trenches that November.

Dear J. - Just a line in answer to your ever welcome letter. Glad to see that all are well. I suppose you saw where our Battalion was in the trenches for a short time. Well it was right in them, only the weather was wet, which made it rather uncomfortable and miserable for beginners like what we were, but we managed to stand the strain of shot and shell all right although it was pretty hot at times. I may tell you we were upset and excited at the beginning, but like every thing else we came used to it, and now we are all back safe and sound in our billets. I want you to give my best thanks to the staff of the old *Impartial Reporter* Office for the cigarettes sent. I will always remember it to them. I am still in the same old spirits. Hope this letter finds you in the best of health. Remember me to all the old staff. Again thanking you for the parcel, I am still enjoying the best of health and am still in the same old spirits. I am your old chum.

J.R.Irvine

This is part of a report in a local paper.

An Enniskillen boy in the 11th Inniskillings writing home says, "the first night we went in, we were attached to a line Battalion and had a good time. During the night a sergeant took me out on a listening patrol and we crept to within about ten yards of the German trenches and had to lie there for about four hours trying to get some information. The second night we had to take our trenches on our own and we were drenched to the very skin, for it rained the whole night. The third day was very quiet, and on the fourth and last our artillery cut the parapets off the German trenches to our right. Sergeant Brown had a narrow escape that day, as after one of our shells had burst in the German lines, a piece of it flew back and fell not a yard from where he was standing."

Goggles for each man in the Battalion had been issued and as a foretaste of future events instructions in rapid mobilisation were received. As if to emphasise the point thirty reinforcements arrived.

On 21st December the Battalion temporarily lost their much loved Commanding Officer Lt. Col. W. F. Hessey. He took over command of the Brigade from Brig. J. Hickman who went on leave. Major The Earl of Leitrim assumed command of the Battalion.

Christmas Day and Boxing Day were holidays and all those men who were not needed for essential duties had a well earned rest. All the usual trimmings and ample Christmas fare being provided, the companies competing with each other to provide the best. There is no doubt the thoughts of home and loved ones were uppermost in the mind of every man.

Mrs. Hessey, wife of Lt. Col. Hessey, commanding the Eleventh said "that the responses which the women of Fermanagh have made to Mrs. Clarke's Plum Pudding Fund Appeal is a magnificent one, and far exceeds our widest expectations. Mrs. Clarke tells me that she has been able to send out a more than ample supply to my husband's Battalion."

They were not to know they would spend another three Christmas days in similar circumstances if they survived.

Chapter 10

A New Beginning

The New Year began with orders being received for two companies to move to Canaples and report to the Royal Engineers. This was all part and parcel of the War; the Infantry being used to help the Engineers' efforts in every way that was practical. Manpower was needed to repair villages, railways, erect hutments and build defences. On arrival at Canaples B and D Companies were in the frustrating position of having no accommodation. They then had to march to Halloy to find billets.

Previously No. 3 platoon commanded by Lt. H. C. Gordon went as an advance party to take over billets for the Battalion. They had a good deal of hard work to do to make them clean and habitable.

On 6th January the remainder of the Battalion arrived in Canaples. This time the billets of the 18th Manchesters were taken over.

The same work continued - repairing and bunking of barns and the construction of horse lines. A large party was also required for woodcutting and D Coy were at Halloy working on a hutting scheme. During this time it appeared that the natural skills were being used in repairing and restoring all the local area.

The only other significant event occurred on 23rd January when two officers and thirty-three men were transferred to 109 Brigade machine-gun Company. These had been formed from men and guns withdrawn from each Battalion. To replace the guns each Battalion was issued with Lewis guns. Eventually there were sixteen Lewis guns in each Battalion.

For the complications of modern warfare specialist training was instituted under brigade arrangements for machine gunners, trench mortar personnel, signallers and non-commissioned officers. Among those transferred was Pte James Quigley from St. Johnston, Co. Donegal.

The good news from a morale point of view was that leave was now authorised for the Battalion at the rate of one man each day.

The local newspapers were full of stories of human interest and there certainly appeared to be no restriction on details published in the early part of the war.

The letter reproduced here gives weight to that fact and information as to who the writers were. These men were detached from the Eleventh for a while on a working party at Le Havre. There are some useful details for an enemy in this letter which was published in the Impartial Reporter in January 1916. The editor - Mr. W. Trimble - had already sent a mouth organ to each platoon. That was sixteen altogether. He did send the writers one as well!

Dear Sir: - As there is a lot of the old 11th Inniskillings at the base, Le Havre, some of them almost knocked out of action, and wish to be remembered to the people of Enniskillen and round Fermanagh, we would be very thankful to some of them if they would kindly oblige them by sending out a mouth organ or two to assist them in raising a little rag time band for a little pass-time in the winter evenings.

All the boys here at present spent a very enjoyable Christmas. Any amount of everything especially cigarettes and tobacco. The most of us have been temporarily employed for a short time at the base, and hope to rejoin our units very shortly in the trenches, and we would all wish very much to be back with some of the old boys again. Wishing everybody a very happy New Year.
Signed - 17283, L. Cpl. W. Elliott; 14103, Drummer R. McVitty; 24462, Gunner W. Cranston; 17232, Pte. R. Little; 21282, Pte. H. Wiggins.
All the knuts from Fermanagh.

In the first week of February there was a Battalion route march which went well and no one dropped out. The Battalion was warned along with the remainder of 109 Brigade to be prepared to move forward. At noon on 7th February the 36th Division took over its first line with 108 Brigade on the right, 107 Brigade on the left and 109 Brigade in reserve. Like their predecessors they marched towards the sound of the guns. During 8th and 9th February the 11th Inniskillings completed two long tiring marches to arrive after midnight at Forceville.

Following two days of routine work the Battalion was then attached to 107 Brigade. The Battalion took over the position of the 11th Royal Irish Rifles. There were two companies - A and C - in the trenches and B and D in Brigade Reserve at Forceville.

There was some enemy activity and Pte J. Dale and Pte J. Gordon were wounded. After four days B and D companies relieved A and C companies in the trenches.

The trenches were very wet and muddy. Although the arrangements of feeding and supply worked well they barely helped to reduce the discomfort of the men in the water-logged trenches.

In ordinary circumstances rations were sent up nightly from the Quartermaster's stores but in particularly difficult times the men existed for their four day spell on what they could carry in.

At Auchonvillers Pte W. Williams was wounded.

At 6 p.m. on 19th February the left of B and D companies received an intense artillery bombardment which lasted for forty-five minutes. The reserve companies stood to until 10 p.m. Then next day A and C companies relieved B and D companies who marched to billets at Mailly Mailett. Pte J. Evans was wounded following the relief.

There was a heavy fall of snow in the last week of February. The Eleventh were marching again - more of those weary marches in snow and mud. The Battalion was relieved by the 8th Bn the Royal Irish Fusiliers. A and C companies marched from the trenches to billets at Forceville. In more snow B and D companies marched from Mailly Maillet also to Forceville.

On the night of 28th February the Eleventh Battalion took over the line held by comrades of their neighbouring county and city - the Derrys. This area had recently been captured from the Germans. The water was deep and gum boots were piled at the end of the communication trench. The men collected them as they went in.

The strength of the Battalion was thirty-one officers and nine hundred and seventy-two other ranks.

Sunday eve.

Dear Mother,

I was wondering if you has received my letters, as I have not had an answer, but perhaps they have gone astray. I enclose an embroidered [handkerchief] as a souvenir from France. I got a supplies to-day from J. Whyte. I got a letter from Martha yesterday and old was telling me that they kids at school were of knitting socks for us. I trust you will write & thank Martha for the one I got. I am getting on fine so far, of course we have to put up with some hardships, but it is all in the game, so we cannot grumble. We are billeted in a small farm, and it is a kind of a "Pa Said Farm" & we all turned kind of an affair, as we are pitched like herring in a barrell but of course that makes us all the warmer at night. I enclose a P.C. for Ruby. I think this is all at present with love to all

from loving Son
J.Q.

Letter from James Quigley. St. Johnston

CHAPTER 11
Distinguished Conduct

The sentries were finding their duties a strain. The need to talk in whispers at night, with weapons at the ready, peering out into the darkness through the barbed wire was very tiring. During the first two days and nights of March there was artillery fire at regular intervals but fortunately no casualties resulted.

Unknown to any of the Inniskillings the Germans were tunnelling underneath with the intention of blowing up the position. At 11.30 p.m. on the 2nd of March the enemy exploded a huge mine in front of the position known as the Redan. This was a small lozenge-shaped area of trenches jutting out from the British line on high ground east of Beaumont Hamel.

It was not more than fifty yards from the German trenches. There were mines there making it a very hazardous place, especially when occupied at night. Very often large work parties were supplied to carry away sandbags of chalk for the miners. Pte Louis Hazlett was on sentry duty outside the Redan when there was a violent explosion injuring several of the tunnellers. He unhesitatingly climbed down into the forty foot shaft. In the gloom he rescued three men who were trapped in the gas-filled mine.

For this gallant and courageous action he was awarded the Distinguished Conduct Medal. The details published in the London Gazette on 15th April 1916 read "For conspicuous initiative when on sentry duty. After he had incapacitated several tunnellers, Private Hazlett descended a forty foot shaft without hesitation and rescued one man, and returned to assist in rescuing others. He has no experience of mining." This was the first award for gallantry made to the Eleventh.

At the time the Brigade and Divisional Commanders also added their congratulations.
The Battalion was relieved by the 15th R. Ir. Fus. at 11 p.m. on the 3rd March and went to rest billets at Forceville.

On 5th March the Battalion embarked on a tough four hour march from Forceville to Mensil. The Battalion were now attached to 108 Brigade in support of 12th R. Ir. Fus. C Company took over Mound Keep.

The next few days saw intermittent shelling of the positions. Our own Artillery shelling the enemy transport on the evening of the 8th March for two hours. Pte T. Hicks was accidentally wounded by rifle fire. Pte E. Brown and S. Mathews also sustained wounds.

On the 10th March Pte Garbutt and Pte J. Kennedy from Glasgow were killed by rifle fire. That night there was a vicious bombardment on the sector to the right of the Battalion from eleven o'clock to midnight. The next night the 14th R. Irish Rifles relieved the 11th Battalion which returned to rest billets at Mensil.

Having had a rest on the Sunday the next two days were occupied by RE Works. This was hard work making dug-outs, propping, carrying away soil and pumping out trenches. Our artillery bombarded Thiepval Wood, beginning at noon for about an hour and a half, in retaliation for the enemy's bombardment a few days earlier.

Capt. J. Boyton, Pte W. Stratton, Pte A. Devine and Pte R. Johnston were all wounded by artillery fire later on the same day.

At 9.30 p.m. the Battalion relieved the 14 R. Ir. Rifles in the trenches. Next day the front line trench received twenty-five mortar shells plus a variety of other shells and remarkably had no casualties.

On St. Patrick's Day, 1916, the Eleventh's front line was shelled in the afternoon and Pte W. Smith from Durham was killed. Pte A. Campbell, Pte T. Brotherstone and Pte S. McIlfatrick were wounded.

During the next few days there was some shelling mainly directed at Hamel. Twenty mortar shells caused the communication trench to collapse and L/Cpl G. Clarke and Pte C. Peoples were wounded.

The weather was still a formidable foe and made life very difficult. The Donegal and Fermanagh men met this hardship and were already establishing an excellent reputation for hard work and steadiness under fire.

The Battalion was again relieved by the 14th Battalion R. I. Rifles during the night of 21st March and returned to rest billets at Mensil. This route was by way of the infamous Jacob's ladder - a communications trench which ran from Mensil village to Hamel - down a forward slope completely exposed to the enemy.

Detailed written orders were always issued for the relief. Those of us today who are concerned with communications and administration will marvel at their contents particularly when we consider the conditions under which they were written, distributed and expedited. They contained details of the order of relief by companies, instructions for guides, tasks for cooks and signallers. Orders for Guards at particular installations were included as well as details for the disposal and accounting for trench stores. A list of the latter had to be given to the Adjutant by 10 a.m. the next day. Each company had to take over any trench work needed to be done e.g. constructing dug-outs and propping.

Details about rations were very specific, particularly if there were detachments working with the Royal Engineers or other supporting arms.

Finally everything had to be clean and tidy in true Inniskilling fashion and Battalion Headquarters in the trenches notified by wire or runner on completion of relief.

The Battalion remained in the line for the remaining days of March. It was a fairly quiet period with a few "whiz bangs" and "oil cans" being fired.

Second Lieutenant Cyril Falls sent this factual but humourous account of a day in the trenches with the 11th Inniskillings to the Impartial Reporter.

It is very dark and very quiet. The officer of the watch moves slowly along the trench. Coming round a traverse he encounters a dim figure, monstrous in a grey goat-skin coat.

"N.C.O. on trench duty, sir. All correct."
"Any word of the patrol yet, Corporal?"
"No, sir, not yet."
"Well, it's a quarter to four and they were due back at three. Hope there's nothing wrong."
"I expect it's all right. There hasn't been a sound."
The officer passes down the line, stopping now and then to speak to a sentry. Then he enters a long, narrow, listening post, running out through the British wire toward the German lines. One of the two sentries posted at the end meets him half-way down.
"The Boche train's in again at the station, sir. We can hear quite plain. The brakes of her was scringein' a minute since. And there's transport up round her."
"Right you are! Get back to your post and listen."

A Howitzer Shell Comes

The officer turns and makes his way down a communication trench to the signal office. He scribbles a message on the form handed to him by the telephonist and hurries back to the fire-trench. There he waits five minutes, ten minutes, a quarter of an hour, kicking his toes against the fire - platform to warm them and bestowing a few extra curses on that oft-cursed instrument, the field telephone. At last - oh, joy, high above his head sounds the wuz-uz-uz-uz of a howitzer shell sailing over, and a few seconds later the roar of its explosion a mile in front.

"Right into the ____ station, I do believe," says the officer to himself, rubbing his hands.
"Hope it got a few of the ____s!"

(It may here be mentioned that there are two words of very frequent occurrence in the trenches, a noun and an adjective. To describe our friend the enemy they are generally used together. If the reader will imagine one or other, or more frequently both, in every sentence spoken, it will be unnecessary to indicate their presence here-after.)

Now the field guns take up the tale, and for the next five minutes the station and the whole village are peppered from end to end with shrapnel. The train is heard backing out in a hurry, the clatter of horses' hoofs at a gallop tells of the transport dispersed, and dimly across the valley come the shouts of the drivers and their officers. One can imagine blood-curdling Boche curses hurled across at the Irish mercenaries. Our friends have, it would seem, 'got it in the neck.' Their gunners, waking up and apparently taking a serious view of the case, proceed to put about forty shells of various calibre into the two villages directly behind our lines.

As things quiet down, the officer of the watch meets a sergeant passing down the trench and informing each sentry that the patrol is in. He looks at his watch. It is ten minutes to five.

'Stand To'

'And you may pass down right and left, sergeant, "stand to," from me.
"Very Good, Sir!"
Then he betakes himself to the dug-out where the other three officers of his company are sleeping on their wire beds, and pokes his head in. From its recesses greets him a delicate scent blended of coke-fumes, goat-skin coats, rubber boots slightly heated, tobacco smoke, and moderately well-washed humanity. One man is snoring lustily, another sitting up and extricating his feet from the sand-bags he had been wearing in order to keep his boots from dirtying the blankets.
"Stand to, you blighters" he remarks amiably, then passed on to the mess dug-

out, and breaks open the box containing the morning's rum. With one jar under his arm and a cup in his hand, he returns to the fire-trench. The dawn is reddening the sky as the men pass to their places in the fire-bays from their dug-outs. They look lovingly on the stone jar as it passes slowly up to them.

The Rum

"I'm a Catch-me-Pal at home, right enough", observes one, "but out here, begob _____" the rest is a gurgle followed by a cough.

The serving out of rum helps to pass for officers and men the chilly and unpleasant hour of morning 'Stand to'. As soon as 'Stand down' had been passed along the line by the Company Commander, the Officer of the Watch, his Watch now over, returns to Company headquarters, pours himself out a coffee-cup full of milk and whiskey - in this sector there are some cows included in 'trench stores', so we luxuriate in fresh milk - and, so with the aid of a cigarette and *La Vie Parisienne* of the week before last, endures till he hears the welcome sizzling of bacon from the kitchen opposite. As we sit down to breakfast, the ration-men or 'mate-carriers' go past with that of the men, field-kettles full of tea and pans of bacon carried in wooden frames, each on the shoulders of two men.

The Quietest Time

Between 'Stand down' - say six o'clock this time of year - and 10 o'clock is the quietest time in the trenches. It is occupied with breakfast, the cleaning of rifles and bombs, and sleep. Unless when the trenches are flooded, when the pumps must be kept going at all hazards, no other work is done. We always believe that the enemy also takes it easy at this time. Just about 'Stand to' he becomes very energetic and obnoxious; the fire from his rifles fixed on various portions of our line increases five-fold, and his machine-guns traverse our parapet. Then smoke begins to ascend from his trenches, and from the next few hours he leaves us more or less alone.

At ten o'clock our day's work begins. A throng of men assembles round the Company Sergeant-Major's dug-out, where he gives out tools and materials and details the various working parties. The 11th pride themselves on their work in the trenches, and boast that they have never yet been in a sector without making a change in it during their stay that the merest tyro could appreciate. Half a dozen small parties are for work in the fire-trench, repairing the traverses and revetting the parapet with rabbit-wire or expanded metal and iron stakes. Another is working on a new dug-out for their section, because the old one is very deep and only one entrance, and has therefore been condemned as unsafe by the Colonel. Yet another party is set to filling sand-bags for a new communication trench. The actual digging of the trench has to be done by night, because it is commanded from the German lines. Even then it is not exactly a pleasing task, for the astute Boche has guessed that there is work in progress, and fires off a belt from a machine-gun along its length every couple of hours.

Boast of the Eleventh

Shortly before this the Battalion Bombing Officer, known to the irreverent as 'Bim-Bom,' has arrived for breakfast. The great man dwells at Headquarters in a palatial dug-out, but deigns to visit his company mealtimes, or rather to take his meals there at his own times. Beaming after a wash and shave following a good night's sleep, he makes us all feel very haggard and tired and dirty. His mouth full of bacon, he lectures us on not keeping our bombs as they ought to be kept, and we promise humbly to amend our ways.

The 11th have another boast besides that of working well in the trenches - that they never lose an opportunity to annoy the enemy. Experience has already taught them that if you lie down to the Boche he walks on your stomach. Half a dozen snipers from each of the companies in the firing-line station themselves at well concealed positions. They have telescopic sights on their rifles, and are a terror to any German that dares show any portion of himself, even if he be a thousand yards away.

The Official Reports

'Bim-Bom' and three or four of his desperadoes go off to fire volleys of rifle-grenades into a German sap-head. Another officer takes a powerful telescope to an observation post, and rakes the trenches in front of us and the ground behind them, noting where work is in progress, the position of dug-outs, paths and trenches to the rear that are evidently much used by night; all of which information will eventually reach the artillery and the machine-gun company, who will, we hope, take action accordingly. In his dug-out, the Company Commander is making out his 'Intelligence Report'. He tells what his patrol last night discovered of the movement of hostile patrols or of the state of the German wire; of the condition of his own wire and the points where his wiring-parties improved it during the preceding night; of the position of Boche snipers and machine-gun emplacements, and the points in the trenches which they have rendered dangerous; of enemy signals by means of coloured rockets and their probable significance; in fact of anything connected with the enemy's movements, dispositions or habits that he; his company officers, his scouts or his sentries have observed in the past 24 hours.

Others are at Work

So the morning and early afternoon pass, pleasantly enough. It is fine weather, our trenches are dry, and we look back, as on an ugly dream, on the days when rain stopped only to give place to snow, and the pumps ceased never day nor night, and we were stuck in the mud and had to be pulled out minus our thigh-boots. Our artillery is wire-cutting, and we have observers in the front line noting where the Boche wire is destroyed, so that by night we may harass him with the fire of Lewis guns and rifles when he attempts to repair the damage. Occasionally our aeroplanes cross the German line, or, more rarely, one of his comes over our own, and then the sky is flecked with the white puffs of bursting shrapnel from the anti-aircraft guns which the airmen seem to treat with complete and well-merited contempt.

After tea and before 'stand to', the Boche is particularly quiet. Two officers are in Company Headquarters writing home, the rest are up in the line. Presently they stroll into the trench. Though the sun is low it is still warm.

A Surprise

'It'll be "stand to" in half-a-hour,' he says. 'Let's go and see if we can strafe a few rats in the old trench before ____'.
The other catches him by the arm.
"Look! Look! Right into the village!"
Against the sky, almost over their heads, a little shell-shaped projectile is sailing by in leisurely fashion. It drops beside a house they can see through the trees. A second later stones, bricks, clods of earth are flying through the air, and there follows a thunderous grinding explosion.

Our old friend, the Boche trench-howitzer, perhaps the most deadly weapon in all his armoury, with a range of over twelve hundred yards, is opening on us. After an interval of a minute and a half, a second shell follows the first. This appears to land in open ground, and the onlookers are relieved. They know that by now every man in the village has had time to take cover. They discuss the direction from which the gun is firing.

Safe in the Cave

"The same old spot, I'll take my oath!" says one. "That's coming from the very place she was pooping from last time. Just about fifty yards back from ___ My God! she's shortening! Run for it. The caves!"

It may be explained that the mess dug-out faces a high bank, out of which is hollowed a cave with several entrances, the abode of a reserve platoon and the Company Signal Office. Into this haven the two officers dash - just in time. There is a tremendous roar as the bomb explodes on the bank above their heads. Some of the shoring supporting the roof cracks and strains ominously, and a shower of chalk falls about the heads of those inside. One of the officers runs out into the trench to watch for the next bomb. The gun evidently takes some time to fire, for there is a regular interval of at least one hundred seconds between shots. He comes back with word that the next is landing almost in the same place. It actually falls into the trench about twenty yards below them, and again comes that ear-splitting roar and a fresh shower of earth and chalk from the roof of the cave.

"Damn it, I'll try and get the artillery on to the blighters!" says the officer, and picks up a block of message forms.

Can't get the Artillery

The message, giving the point from which the gun is believed to be firing, necessarily takes some time to write, partly because the shock of each bomb exploding puts out all the candles in the cave, and several more have burst, some close at hand, some further down the trench, before it is handed to the telephonist. Then the officer goes back to the mouth of the cave. After three more explosions, he heard the voice of one of the signallers behind him.

"We can't get the artillery, sir, or headquarters. The wires is broke."

The officer says that which he considers warranted by the occasion.

"And headquarters won't know what the deuce is happening to us," he goes on. "Look here, someone must scoot out as soon as the next bursts, and run like blazes for it. Tell them we're all right, but that we're getting it pretty warm, and that the gun is firing from the old spot."

A Plucky Volunteer

A volunteer at once steps forward, and rushes out while the earth thrown up by the next bomb is still pattering down into the trench. In a moment he is back.

"Please, sir, there's no trench at all left below us there. Sure the whole of it's levelled out and filled with lumps that'd take ye half an hour to climb over. I'll try if ye like ___."

Bang! The next bomb bursts just about where the messenger would have been had he started on his errand.

The officer feels that even swearing is no good now. He turns to the telephonist.

"Certain you can't get any of the companies?" he demands. "All the wires gone? Then, by Jove, someone must try the other way up the trench!"

The boy at the telephone slips the receiver-band from his head and hands it to a comrade.

"They're all cut, sir, right enough. I'll run away up the other way, down Dolly's Brae and across the open. I'll not be two minutes!"

The Last Shot

He waits for the next to burst, and runs up the trench. But he need not have hurried, for this, the 25th shot, is the last, and those in the cave are left to sally forth after a few minutes and survey the damage. The trench for a hundred yards down is a trench no more, and all about are holes 10 feet deep and 12 across. Three men, who have run down from the firing-line are surveying the mess dug-out, the door of which is filled in, horror-stricken, and one is calling to his God that 'the officers is buried in there, so they are'.

So ends the 'strafe,' for our artillery decides not to retaliate just at present, though a promise is sent to us from the 'heavies' that in due time they will plough up the whole sector from which the howitzer has been firing. We proceed to count the damage. The casualties are: one man suffering from shock - he was knocked down stunned, and half buried - one man with a piece of lead the size of a pea in his calf who returns to duty next day, and one particularly fine buck rat. The officers' dug-out takes some time to re-open and repair. Our dinner is an hour late, and the beef is full of grit.

That is all. The telephone is working as well as it ever works - which is not saying much - within half an hour. One hundred men from the support company, working nearly all night, dig out the trench, and by morning light there is no sign

B.E. Force.
16. 3. 16.

Dear Mother,
I had 2 parcels from Father just the other day — thanks very much, my formamint are about finished & I had asked Minnie for some but she sent formalin, so I'm pretty well stocked now. I have been & am kept pretty busy but I'm in very good health & am keeping quite fit. We had another big scrap with guns, you would believe how little the men trouble about shells, you should hear them saying "awa man those Germans have got past the night again & got too much beer. At home they talk about German shooting, & we do here too but the shooting of our anti aircraft guns is superb. I watched one of the German aircraft to day having as hot a time as you could wish for. Capt Boyton of

Lt. Henry Gallaugher's letter regarding German shells.

of the Boche handiwork. A box of detonators, the property of 'Bim-Bom', has disappeared from the shelf in our dug-out, and we are left in pleasing uncertainty as to where they now abide. But the Boche trench-howitzer officer probably thinks he has exterminated us, and we feel sure he has been awarded the Iron Cross.

Writing to his mother in March Lt. Henry Gallaugher described the morale of the men during shell fire. He gives a humourous glimpse of their reaction in the vernacular of Donegal. Later on in his letter he gives a graphic account of the duties of a transport office when the Eleventh came out of the trenches. His letter is reproduced for the vivid picture it portrays.

On the last day of March 109 Infantry Brigade Orders contained the details of the award of the Distinguished Conduct Medal to Pte Hazlett. The Divisional Commander also added his congratulations.

CHAPTER 12

An Unfortunate Accident

This period began sadly with a tragic accident on 2nd April at a place known as Stonebridge. A grenade was accidentally dropped into a shelter killing Pte W. Clarke of Glasgow and Pte J. Armstrong from Newtownbutler. Ptes Doherty, Eades, Fleming and McCrea were wounded.

The Battalion was relieved by 14th Royal Irish Rifles and returned to rest billets at Mensil. Next day the enemy shelled Mensil and in the late afternoon one shell wounded several soldiers: Ptes M. McFarren, J. Gillan, R. McConnell and H. McIlroy.

During the next couple of days the Battalion was employed on R.E. work. On the 6th the enemy heavily shelled the village in the evening for about two hours. This time there were no casualties but some houses in the village were damaged. The work in repairing billets and making good all other facilities was heavy and demanding. The Battalion were in the trenches again on the late evening of the 8th April. The usual trench routine continued. C.S.M. Blake of D Coy was wounded by rifle fire. L/Cpl Middlemas was killed and Ptes Briggs and Melanophy wounded by shell fire.

The Battalion returned to Mensil. A Company was at Mound Keep. On 14th April Lt. Col. Hessey took over command of 109 Inf. Brigade during the absence Brig. T. Hickman. Command of the Battalion devolved to Capt. W. T. Sewell as no other officer more senior was there at that time.

Next day Ptes D. McLaughlin and R. Derby were wounded at Mensil by machine-gun fire, the enemy being very active in the area.

Later that day Major the Earl of Leitrim rejoined from leave and recruiting duties and assumed command of the Battalion.

Lt. Henry Gallaugher had written home to his mother at Balleighan, near Manorcunningham in Donegal, to say that he was leaving the transport platoon to become second in command of C Coy. He stated that everything ran sweetly in transport. He observed pertinently how every soldier needed to know how to look after himself before he was any use to others. He stated how wet the weather was and how everyone felt annoyed at being recalled from leave early.

nothing, mind you rather like C. Coy not that I prefer it to B. Of course I would rather have our own old coy but the other is quite good & Capt Ballantine is alright. I shall let you know as things work out. I am rather sorry that I'm leaving the transport as everything connected with it ran so smoothly & one had absolutely no trouble. Everyone knew their job, & I think they know pretty well that an ordinary soldier must first be able to look after himself before he is any use to any one & with a bit of training they soon learn that; if he does not look after himself he soon becomes a burden to the Government. It is pretty wet just now out here. I do trust that the weather has taken up at home & that it will let the work well forward

Part of Lt. H. Gallaugher's letter home.

During the next week the situation remained static and there were a few casualties from machine-gun fire. The Battalion moved again with A Coy in South Antrim villas, C Coy to Authvile B, D and H.Q. Coys in Martinsart Wood. Pte C. Mumford of C. Coy was wounded at Will Bridge Authvile. On 24th April the Battalion relieved the 9th Battalion (Tyrones) of the Inniskillings. Three platoons of each company being in the front line with one platoon per company in reserve. Before the end of April there were more casualties from Artillery fire; these included Sgt J. McClure, Ptes J. McKelvie, J. Adams, Pte J. McGowan. 2nd. Lt. P. Hall of St. Johnston, County Donegal died of wounds.

April ended with the Battalion being relieved by 14 R.I. Rifles. H.Q. Coy A and C Coy were in rest billets at Martinsart Wood. B Coy in tents in the same place. D Coy in billets in Martinsart.

Apart from casualties resulting from enemy action morbidity was low and the Battalion had a strength of thirty-three officers and nine hundred and sixty-seven other ranks.

CHAPTER 13

Dummy Trenches

In the grand scale of the planning things were changing. Preparations had to be made for a very ambitious effort to redress the present situation and end the stalemate of the trenches.

The 11th Inniskillings found the beginning of May in the Martinsart area relatively normal. There were surely frequent thoughts of home - of the corn beginning to spring and the hawthorn starting to blossom. During this time they earned the name of 'God's Own' because their casualties were relatively light.

Orders were received for the Battalion to change station following relief by the 13th R. I. Rifles. The 11th marched to Varennes through Hedauville getting there shortly after midnight. Here they relieved the 15th R. I. Rifles.

On the 10th of May the Battalion started to practise attacks. All this had to be gone into in the greatest detail so that each man would know exactly what was expected of him. Large areas of Dummy Trenches were laid out for this purpose. As far as possible they were replicas of the enemy's construction. Details were obtained from air photos and other intelligence information.

This form of training continued for over a week. Route marches and other training interspersed this activity and culminated with Brigade training in the middle of the month. There was little entertainment for the soldiers during any recreation periods. There were some little cafes and bars but they were in pretty run down condition.

Lt. Col. Hessey had returned to assume command on Sunday 14th of May and Divine Service was also held. The Earl of Leitrim was admitted to the Divisional Rest station at the end of the third week of May.

Arduous training continued. The intention being that the artillery would plaster the German lines for five days with the heaviest bombardments ever attempted in war. On Z day the infantry would attack. When the German lines were smashed the cavalry would break through and in classic cavalry style attack the enemy's flanks and rear.

On the dummy trenches all the different strong points and lines were given names of places at home to enable the men to remember them clearly.

The Eleventh were also now learning the rudiments of a new battle technique known as the 'creeping barrage'. This had never been used before. The first essential was that the artillery smash up the hostile wire so the attacking infantry got through and the second was to pulverise the enemy's front line to diminish any strong resistance to the attack.

Concentrated artillery fire would be directed initially at a point about the middle of 'No Man's Land' and move very slowly forward. The infantry would leave their trenches precisely at the start of the barrage and move forward with it keeping as near to it as possible.

That was the theory of what the men were now training for but in practice the grim reality would be a fearsome consequence.

For the rest of the month the Eleventh trained hard with typical Inniskilling enthusiasm, encompassing Stokes Mortar demonstrations, Brigade operations and other skills. There still had to be supplied working parties for the R. E. and other duties. This was hard physical work.

Capt. W. T. Sewell again took command when Lt. Col. Hessey went on leave. A draft of sixty-one men joined late in the month. There was even time to find an afternoon for the Brigade Sports on 27th of May.

The weather turned wet again as the month was closing and training in the dummy trenches was intermittent for the last two days in May.

This page from the Roll Book of L.O.L. 1927 is an unusual record. It shows that about a quarter of the members were serving in the Army in 1916. A number of these served in the Eleventh. Wm. Flackes was the father of the late W. D. Flackes the well known political broadcaster and writer. Other known members of the Eleventh were Wm. T. McClintock and Robert Dinsmore both of whom were killed at the Somme.

BURT FAITH DEFENDERS,
LOYAL ORANGE LODGE, No. 1927. A.D. 1916

All serving in Kitchener Army

No.	Name	Address
56	Sam¹ Allen	Castlequarter Inch
57	John Knott	Coshquin Bridge End
58	James Austin	Burt Bridge End
59	Rob¹ Anderson	Springtown Derry
60	William Walker	Coshquin Upper
61	Rob¹ Dinsmore	Ephormican Hulp P.O.
62	John Kee	" "
63	Andrew Dinsmore	Birdstown Burnfoot P.O.
64	Andrew S. Robinson	Gortormican Inch
65	Geo. McGowan	" "
66	James Dinsmore	Lenamore
66	Tom McClay	Eirshaughmoye Burnfoot P.O.
67	Sam¹ Lynch	Lovett Bridge End
68	Wm. J. McClintock	Fahaugh (Killed in Action)
69	Jos. Crockett	Elagh Beg Burnfoot
70	Tom Taccles	Gunamaddy Newtowncunningham
71	Rob¹ Bell (Dead)	Drumacross Burnfoot P.O.

CHAPTER 14
Tunnelling, Digging and Shelling

The Eleventh started the month by supplying three companies as working parties for the Royal Engineers. They were engaged in preparing shelters and positions for French Artillery which had just arrived in the area. Assistance was given for tunnelling in Thiepval Wood. Tunnelling was hard and dangerous work. There was no glamour in working underground. There was very real danger from gas and injury by falling debris caused by shell fire. Water was everywhere slopping through the tunnels.

The purpose of tunnelling was to enable large quantities of explosives to be placed at strategic points near the German defences. Tunnels were over eighty feet underground opening into huge chambers which were filled with ammoral usually in tins.

Preparation for the forthcoming great attack continued and Brigade operations continued on the practice trenches. This meant that each individual was toiling extremely hard considering that the working parties continued as well.

All this activity continued speedily in the second week of June. Divisional Concentration Operations took place at Baizieux. On the ninth of June Lt. Col. Hessey was appointed to command 110 Infantry Brigade. His distinguished career continued and he became a Major General gaining the D.S.O. and Bar and the Russian Order of St. Stanislas.

Command of the Eleventh devolved to Capt. Sproule Myles from Ballyshannon. This was the first time an Ulster Volunteer officer with no previous military experience was in command.

If success was to be assured then the training carried out on the elaborate system of dummy trenches was vital. These were marked out with spade and plough near Clairfaye Farm and the Eleventh were there in the second week of June. By now all the men realised something very big was about to happen.

The result of all this was that each man knew his task so well that he pushed on to his objective when his leaders had fallen.

The Eleventh got a new Commanding Officer when Major C. H. Brush joined

B.E.F.
27th June 1916.

My Dear Mother,

We are just moving out to the line tonight & I expect this is the last letter you may get for a bit, of course I shall write (D.V.) at the first opportunity. I am just going down now to see all Nob & I only wish I was going in with them of course it makes very little difference who you go with in our Bn, but the local chaps always come first. We had a very nice little service yesterday evg & had communion, Rev H. Wright & I must say he has always been very nice & friendly to all the boys. I am awfully sorry that our County seems to be included in Home Rule but I don't see how we can better it much, & I would not like to be at home loafing & this going on. & now dear Mother I must say "Goodbye" & may our Heavenly Father watch over all the dear ones at home & keep us all in the way wherein we go & be with us & bless us. With very best love to all at home.

Ever your affect Son
Henry.

Lt. Henry Gallaughers letter prior to the Somme.

from the Tenth Inniskillings and took over from Capt. Myles. This was on the 12th June and the Rev. A. Spence was also attached on the same date.

Work and training continued. Two members of A Coy - Pte. H. Carruthers and Pte. R. Eades - were wounded by Artillery Fire at the south west corner of Thiepval Wood.

The paraphernalia of war was all around them now. Artillery ammunition was piled at the roadsides and everywhere men were working. The weather was hot and they sweated in their dust covered uniforms. Much work was done at night to conceal the activity.

The infantry would assemble in Thiepval Wood prior to attack. Joe Wallace noted how hard the horses worked but he felt they were as well cared for as on any farm at home.

The next day 18th June the Eleventh received orders that they would attack after an artillery bombardment of the German positions. The bombardment was planned to last for six days. These days were lettered T. U. V. W. X. Y. On Z day the attack was to begin.

These orders were received on the anniversary of the Battle of Waterloo where the Inniskillings had been decimated holding the centre of the line. They would receive the same fate in a few days time.

On the same day several men of C Coy's working party were wounded by Artillery fire at the south west corner of Thiepval Wood. They were Cpl. C. Hutchinson Ptes. W. Spiers, R. McDonald and J. Cochrane. Three days later Ptes. Wilson and Murray became shell shock casualties at the same place.

On June 23rd, T Day, the Eleventh moved to the huts at Forceville taking them over at nine o'clock in the evening.

On June 24th the devastating bombardment of the German lines began. The Eleventh were going about their work as always. They were carrying out all the tasks given to them. However, the noise of the guns could not be ignored. In fact the noise could actually be heard in England. The guns would fire continually until the attack.

On Sunday June 25th the Rev. A. Spence conducted Divine Service for all those who could be spared from essential duties. The constant heavy bombarding of the

Artillery was an awesome background noise to the simple act of worship. They all took comfort from the service not knowing what the next few days would bring for them individually. It was raining continually.

On June 27th the Eleventh marched from Forceville to Martinsart. This was a march in very wet and windy conditions. The roads were rutted and very muddy. The first platoon left Forceville at nine-thirty and the last platoon arrived in Martinsart ten minutes before midnight. Everyone was soaked to the skin and highly annoyed that the fine weather had broken. They were very weary having carried all their kit which weighed seventy pounds or more. The enemy reacted to the heavy bombardment and fired twenty shells into Martinsart but this time there were no casualties.

It was on June 28th that the Eleventh received orders that the attack originally planned for that day was postponed. This was because of the dreadful weather.

In the usual military way the lettering of the days had to be altered. The original Z day became YI followed by YII day and then the day after that became Z day on which the attack would be launched. Late in the evening of that day the Eleventh marched from Martinsart to Thiepval Wood to relieve the 9th Inniskillings. The relief was completed ten minutes before midnight and the front line trenches were taken over.

Thiepval Wood was a place which would be known in every home in Ulster and it was here that the Eleventh remained for the next two days. Although the enemy was being constantly shelled, Thiepval Wood was a most uncomfortable place to be as he retaliated. During June 29th many shells landed on the Eleventh's position. These included tear shells. From 3.00 a.m. to 5.00 a.m. there was an intense bombardment by the enemy. He directed fire at all the approaches to Thiepval Wood and assembly trenches at Gordon Castle. This was a nasty morning for everyone. It was still cold and damp. Morale was severely tested by the shelling and the sight of wounded men being carried off by stretcher.

Sgt. T. Willis and Pte. J. McMaster were shell shocked. Ptes. J. Simpson and Pte. J. Stewart were killed. L. Cpl. W. Richardson, Pte. H. McIlroy and Pte. J. White were wounded.

Throughout the day the shelling was intermittent and there were bursts of machine-gun fire from Thiepval village. During all this the front line trench was held by three double sentry posts and two Lewis Guns. The remainder of the Eleventh were in the forward assembly trenches. All that day the men strove hard to keep the communication trenches open. They repaired ramps and improved the assembly trenches.

The night of June 29th was nerve wracking with more shelling.

Early in the morning of June 30th the enemy laid down a fierce bombardment between three and five o'clock.

In spite of these great dangers work continued on the same lines as the previous day to improve the positions. The enemy shelled Gordon Castle and the rear assembly trenches with a hail of tear shells. At noon two men were killed and five wounded.

This front line company was withdrawn in the afternoon and kept in the assembly trenches. They were replaced by four sections of bombers who were also detailed to go forward with the 9th Inniskillings.

The rest of the Eleventh were placed in the assembly trenches in the afternoon. All the material and stores needed for the Advance was distributed amongst the platoons. All arrangements for the Advance were completed before dawn.

A very tense night was spent in this position. Some were seen looking at photographs of loved ones and reading letters from home. Last minute letters were also written.

The strength on that day was Officers thirty-eight and Other Ranks nine hundred and ninety-one.

These letters reflect the recognition and appreciation of the hard work and perseverance of the men of the Eleventh in this memorable year.

The following is a copy of a letter received by the Commanding Officer from Major General O. S. Nugent, Commanding 36th Division, on the 24.6.16.

"H.Q. 36th Divn.
23rd June 1916.

I wish to thank your Battalion through you for the way in which they have worked during the past weeks. From my own observation and from reports received from all sources, I think that officers and men deserve the highest credit for the good honest work they have put in. Where all have worked well as had been the case, it may seem invidious to select one particular Battalion for special praise, but the 11th Rl. Innis. Fus. have earned it from everyone who has worked with them. Will you please thank the Battalion from me and tell them that I wish them the best of luck.

Yours sincerely,
(Sd) Oliver Nugent

The following is a copy of a congratulatory letter received from G.O.C. 36th, Division through Official channels:-

The G.O.C. wishes to express his great satisfaction with the good work performed by the 11th R. Innis. Fus. Parties from this Battalion were found for work on the shelters of the newly arrived French Batteries, also for assisting the Tunnellers in THIEPVAL WOOD and for carrying up R.E., stores. From all three sources reports were received as to the exceptionally good and hard work performed by this Battalion. Success in trench warfare is so largely dependent upon hard work in connection with the preparations for the offensive that it is difficult to exaggerate the value of really good work done in this respect. Please inform the C.O. of the Battalion of the contents of this letter.

The Brigadier General in forwarding the above letter of commendation from the G.O.C. Division wishes to offer his personal congratulations to you and all ranks of the Battalion on the good reports earned by its working parties. The Brigadier would like you to let all Ranks know of the Divisional Commander's appreciation of their good work.

CHAPTER 15
The Somme

It was a clear and sunny morning on July 1st when the Eleventh left their assembly trenches and took over the trenches of the 9th Inniskillings at 7.20 a.m. This was a departure from the normal tactic of a dawn attack.

There was an inspiration in the date to all the men of the Inniskilling Regiment. The anniversary of the Battle of the Boyne - the day on which King William had appointed them his Guards and the first engagement in which they had fought as Regulars.

The Eleventh were determined to show they were worthy of the Regiment in which they had enlisted.

This was their first battle and they were filled with fervour to prove their mettle.

The many hundreds of guns were ranged as one battery. The heavy guns of great calibre were so numerous that they more than doubled the artillery effect of the field guns. Fifteen inch howitzers squatted in surrounding fields and twelve inch guns reared their enormous necks from the streets of Albert. At 6.30 a.m. an intense hurricane bombardment from the Stokes mortars heralded the attack.

The task of the Eleventh was to support the 9th Inniskillings in the attack. On the left were the 10th Inniskillings with the 14th R. Ir. Rifles in support. The Brigade had to attack one of the best defended positions of the German front line. The third or Lisnaskea line of these trenches was the objective. It was reached - but at such a terrible sacrifice of men - nothing was won but glory.

The bugle sounded and A and D Coys led the way over the parapet at 7.30 a.m. They were immediately exposed to the heavy barrage raining in on the front line and machine-gun fire coming from Thiepval village area. A Coy suffered very severely. D Coy reached its objective at the Crucifix.

All the companies suffered terribly. Most of the officers and N.C.O.s were casualties before reaching the Sunken Road. This road got its name because for many generations the farmers simply scraped away the muddy top soil to make a harder surface for cart tracks. In time this became a narrow sunken road nearly twenty feet deep and was an ideal communication trench.

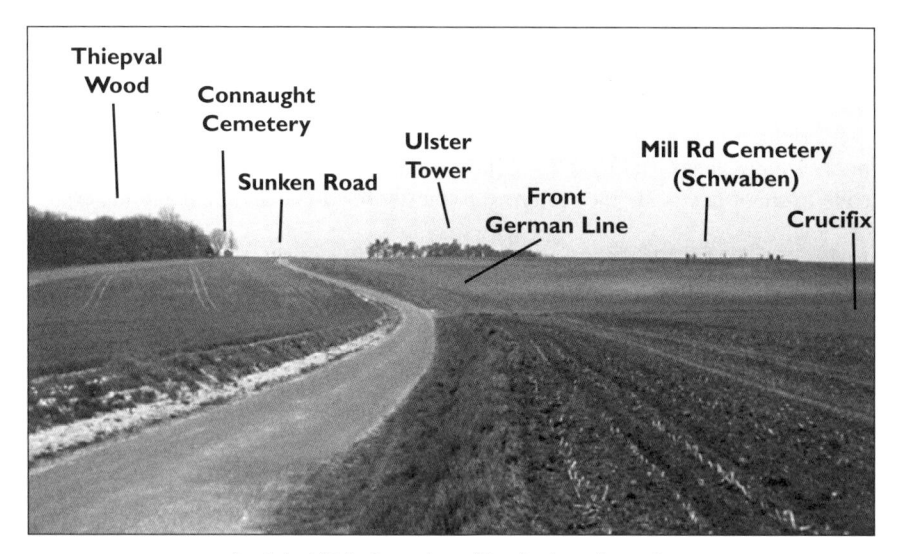

1st July 1916 - Location of beginning of attack.

Led by Capt. W. T. Sewell the Eleventh pushed on to the A line and crossed it. Calling on the remainder of his men to follow him at this point Capt. Sewell was seen to fall, fatally wounded. The situation was grim and the glinting line of the Eleventh's bayonets was thinning fast.

Lt. Frank Gunning, an old Portora boy from Willoughby Place Enniskillen, had been commissioned from that excellent school for junior officers the 7th Royal Dublin Fusiliers. He had served at Gallipoli and was sent home with dysentery. On recovery he went to the 6th Inniskillings and then transferred to the Eleventh.

He was leading the Enniskillen platoon when a bullet took off one of his fingers. As he was binding it up his men urged him to go back to the dressing station. Insisting that his place was with them he refused and went on until a shell extinguished his bright and noble spirit. Men who survived and returned often spoke in the highest terms of his courage and how he led them in the face of heavy fire.

Only one officer was left with the survivors. This was Lt. Henry Gallaugher from Balleighan near Manorcunningham in Co. Donegal. He led them on to their objective the Crucifix. Some men remained here to consolidate the position.

C.S.M. Bullock led the remaining men on to the 'C' line. He dealt with several Germans on the way single-handedly. He was later awarded the M.C. for his courageous action.

No significant opposition was encountered entering the 'B' line. The Germans quickly threw up their hands.

Lt. Henry Gallaugher quickly took command of the situation and had the communication trenches leading to the Crucifix barricaded. He ordered fire steps to be made to shoot from. He then returned to the 'A' line to collect men and material.

On arrival he found part of the 'A' line occupied by the Germans. He quickly organised a bombing party. He noticed Germans firing on the wounded and got into a shell hole with Pte. Toland. He shot six German snipers with his orderly's rifle. His resolute action cleared the enemy from the trenches on his right. He then erected a barricade which he left in the charge of Lance Corporal Porterfield and six men.

All around was absolute confusion, noise and destruction. Lt. Gallaugher realised he had to report the perilous position to Bn. H.Q. This message did not get through - but so often as is the case in the fog of war - arrived elsewhere, namely with the 9th Inniskillings.

At one o'clock Lt. Gallaugher sent another message which eventually arrived at 109 Brigade around three o'clock. This message stated: 'We have a large number of prisoners in the German trenches but are unable to get them across owing to there being too few men to escort them and also that the machine-gun barrage is still very heavy in No Man's Land. The work of clearing the enemy's front lines is continuing'.

The Commanding Officer was in great difficulty. Lt. Col. Brush - with the other Commanding Officers in the Brigade - had been ordered not to lead his men in the attack. He was to command and control the attack from Bn. H.Q. in the trenches. This was to be done by telephone, signal flags, runners and scouts. The sheer volume of the German fire made this system of communication almost impossible. The result of having the Commanding Officer at Battalion Headquarters meant the troops in the battlefield lacked specific direction. Reports of the situation did not get back to the brigade headquarters. Had support been requested, more ground taken in the brave attack would possibly have been held.

All the signallers who went forward in the attack with telephones and flags were immediately killed or wounded. Throughout the day Lt. Col. Brush tried continually to get in touch with the forward troops by runners, scouts or signallers but they were all wounded except one. It was a nightmare situation not being able to communicate with his remaining soldiers out in front. He had no idea of the situation and could only expect the worst.

That afternoon there was further confusion caused by men retiring on the left of the Eleventh. German prisoners were also mixed up among them. For a time the situation was serious and the front line trenches were not occupied. An energetic group consisting of Capt. Moore, Lt. Gordon and R.S.M. Bleakley of the Eleventh got command of the situation and positioned the retiring soldiers in the assembly trenches. Capt. Mulholland of 14 R.I.R. helped in this position.

It was very difficult to understand the precise situation; further confusion being added by the presence of prisoners and more surrendering Germans coming in over the parapet. R.S.M. Bleakley quickly organised a party to occupy the front line. A little bugler of sixteen years brought in five prisoners to the R.S.M. at this stage.

By now Lt. Gallaugher realised the terrible situation the Eleventh were in. He was the only officer who had not been killed or wounded. He collected all the available men who were in the A trench and surrounding shell holes and led them forward to the Crucifix. None of these men were from the Eleventh as the Donegal and Fermanagh men had all gone forward.

All around was horror and chaos. The air was filled with coloured smoke - yellow, black and brown. It was choking everyone. Some men in other units had been told the attack would be like a morning stroll. There is no evidence that this was the thinking in the Eleventh.

In carrying out this risky task he came into contact with several parties of Germans whom he killed. He also carried in a wounded officer 2nd Lt. Jackson from near the enemy's wire.

Having rallied all the men he could, Lt. Gallaugher met up with Major Peacock of the 9th Inniskillings and came under his command. They held their position in very grave circumstances until very late that evening. Some years later Major Peacock was murdered in the South of Ireland by the I.R.A.

The Eleventh were hard pressed. Early in the afternoon there was a danger that supplies of water and ammunition would run out. In the attack each man carried a full water bottle and several bandoliers of ammunition. As well as this they carried a pack with their personal kit, mills bombs, a shovel and in some cases a roll of barbed wire.

Pte. J. Hunter got separated from his comrades but he joined a platoon of another Battalion. He got to the enemy's front line with only four men. He held out there for eight hours as long as his bombs lasted. He knocked out a machine-gun and took seven prisoners. He was later awarded the D.C.M.

R.S.M. Bleakley and Lt. Gordon worked tirelessly all day. They organised parties of ammunition and water carriers. They succeeded in getting water across to the enemy's A line. R.S.M. Bleakley was a formidable character. His niece, Miss Jean Bleakley, told the writer that he had a son in the Eleventh and he was treated strictly the same as all the other soldiers. Miss Bleakley said that her uncle was a small dapper man and perhaps a little bit of a martinet.

The War Diary says "Lt. Gordon also arranged carrying parties for the wounded and during the early morning of 2nd July, with the assistance of C.Q.M.S. Johnston brought up rations for the Battalion to the assembly trenches".

This very difficult situation persisted in spite of a bombardment on the right flank which had been organised to try to relieve them.
The whole traffic control system had broken down. Capt. Moore and R.S.M. Bleakley with doughty Inniskilling determination took control of the situation. They stood on the parapet for long hours and directed the arriving support troops to climb out of the trench into the open. This left the way clear for the continuous stream of wounded being carried back. R.S.M. Bleakley was awarded the M.C. Lt. Knight who was the Bombing Officer was indefatigable in keeping up the supply of bombs and clearing the communication trenches.

The regimental stretcher bearers were extremely hard pressed. They worked to the limit of exhaustion and beyond. The lack of R.A.M.C. stretcher bearers and stretchers at this point - and for whatever reason - made the task much worse, particularly when getting wounded from the Regimental Aid Post to the collecting point. Hence the Regimental stretcher bearers were used for this additional work.

Over one thousand casualties were brought to the Eleventh's Regimental Aid Post. Capt. Crosbie and his helpers worked in very trying conditions at Elgin Avenue for five days and five nights.

George Bruce from Derrygonnelly was a stretcher bearer with D Coy. Right from the start of the battle he was employed in the terrible task of bringing in the wounded. He recalled many years later that his trousers and puttees were sodden with blood.

Willie Eames M.M. from Springfield was a stretcher bearer. While bringing in the wounded he found the body of his brother Hugh.

The heroic work of Capt. Crosbie and the regimental stretcher bearers saved many lives at the time. To have recovered so many wounded preventing exposure and further injury was a magnificent feat.

Such was the organisation in the Regimental Aid Post that having had their wounds dressed the men got cigarettes, cocoa or soup.

For all this exhausting work, great care and skill Capt. Crosbie was subsequently awarded the M.C.

The hoary headed Quartermaster Lt. J. Firth worked unfailingly to send up supplies of food and water. The water supply tank at Elgin Avenue had been wrecked by a shell.

This is part of Capt. Crosbie's report which he recorded after the battle. It conveys an epic picture of the situation:

The Stretcher Bearers worked night and day until we were relieved bringing wounded back from the Sunken Road, no man's land and the wood under continual shell and machine-gun fire.

We located many wounded men in dug-outs and holes in the front line which our stretcher bearers carried in.

The difficulty in keeping the post clear of wounded was our great trouble as there seemed a great want of both R.A.M.C. Stretcher Bearers and Stretchers, so that on several occasions we had to resort to using the Regimental Stretcher Bearers to evacuate wounded to the collecting post which was great hardship on them. All wounded got hot cocoa or soup and cigarettes when they were dressed, for which they were very grateful.

I wish specially to mention the gallant work done by L. Corpl. Cooper, Pte. Megaghy, Pte. Toland, Pte. Brown, Pte. Elliott of 'A' Coy and Pte. Wilson of 'C' Coy, Pte. Robb 'B' Coy and Pte. Fenwick, 'D' Coy.

These men worked continually, Corporal Cooper remaining in the trenches eight hours after the Battalion was relieved to bring in a wounded man from the Front Line Trench.

The great assistance given by Lieutenant Gavin, 14th Royal Irish Rifles made it possible to cope with the enormous number of cases which were dealt with. He went on several occasions to the dug-outs in the front line and located many wounded, and although his feet and ankles were swollen with the continual standing, still continued his work.

Captain Picken also worked with splendid pluck and devotion.

The Orderlies and men of 14th R.I.R. and 10th R. In. F. in conjunction with my men gave very great assistance.

At one period the congestion at the Aid Post became so great that I sent up to Colonel Brush to ask for assistance to evacuate wounded. He sent 2nd Lt. Hanna who collected a number of men and gave me valuable assistance in clearing the Communication Trenches.

(Sd.) D.E. Crosbie, Capt. R.A.M.C.
M.O. i/c 11th (S) Bn. Rl. Innis. Fus.

In his report the Commanding Officer refers to the hard work of Lt. McCorkill and Cpl. Warren of the Transport Section.

The Orderly room staff consisting of Sgt. Beatty, Cpl. McDougal and L/Cpl. F. Kee did excellent work. Ptes Hunter and Smith were invaluable and never failed in delivering their messages.

The Eleventh now held on in this very grim position with D Coy at the Crucifix and the remainder distributed in the C line. The estimated casualties were six hundred by mid morning. Throughout that terrible day they held on with their ranks very depleted but their spirit undaunted. Small groups beat off German attacks throughout the night. The War Diary recorded that the Eleventh had been in the line for six months. "When not actually holding the front line have been supplying working parties and even this did not seem to dampen their ardour."

The Eleventh were ordered out of the line on July 2nd and returned to Martinsart Wood. On July 3rd the Eleventh arrived at Hedauville at tea time.

That night Capt. W. Moore, Lt. H. Gallaugher and twenty men volunteered to go back to Thiepval Wood. From there they searched No Man's Land and returned safely having rescued twenty-eight wounded men. For all his daring Lt. Gallaugher was awarded the D.S.O.

Next night a small party under Capt. Crosbie the M.O. and Lt. G.M. Irvine went back for the same purpose. They were unable to leave the front line as an attack by our troops was imminent and had to abandon the venture.

The Eleventh had suffered very severely on July 1st. Scores of men were casualties and among them was Stewart Buchanan from Burt. He had been last seen alive sitting wounded at the edge of a large shell hole and he had killed six Germans. There is no exact record of his fate. He has no known grave. His name is recorded on the Thiepval memorial. Lesley Bell told the writer that the hospital which he was in a few days later was filled with men from the Eleventh.

The day, which in the minds of some of the men linked the date to the Battle of the Boyne, had not given the expected good outcome.

There were many wounded still lying in No Man's Land. The arrival of search parties and stretcher bearers was an almost miraculous sight.

Now, the Eleventh, weary and very badly mauled tried to get organised and take stock of the situation.

Altogether the information known on July 3rd showed that five hundred and seventy seven men were killed, wounded or missing. A total of fifteen officers were in the same categories. The strength of the four rifle companies coming out of the trenches after the battle totalled two hundred and fifty-one men.

Given the numbers that went in to the battle on the morning of July 1st the feelings of the survivors were sombre indeed. The roll call was scant. Joe Wallace recalled the silence which lasted among the men for a few hours in the aftermath. They thought of their fallen and wounded comrades. They thought of home - of families making hay and of the sound of the corncrake in the meadows of Donegal and Fermanagh.

Soon many of these homes would receive the dreaded buff envelope bearing the tragic news.

What made these men go on in such a murderous fire? Was it their fervent Ulster determination, Regimental pride and training or in the personal loneliness of the individual his desperate desire not to be found wanting? They had done everything expected of them and more.

Shortly after the battle an unnamed soldier of the Eleventh penned these lines and sent them to the Impartial Reporter.

A SOLDIER'S LAMENT

In Memoriam - Thiepval

(For the Impartial Reporter)

The morning mists had lifted not by that dark flowing stream.
The summer sun was peering through, with radiant early gleam,
A gentle breeze was sighing through Thiepval's leafless trees,
On that July morn which should adorn the Ulster Irish name.

The voice of nature was not there, the birds and bees sang not;
The landscape's beauty blasted, with withering shell and shot.
The music was the roar of guns, the fragrance weeping smoke,
As the last half hour, the thunderous shower, the leaden volley broke.

Beyond the Ancre flowed its way, whispering its ancient song
That 'Men may come, and men may go, but I go on and on',
How true its singing seemed to be on that fair summer's day.
When from east and west, and of Ireland's best were gathered for the fray.

Hearts beat expectant, courage breathed with every drawing breath,
None faltered in the supreme hour, though fraught with ghastly death;
Shoulder to shoulder comrades stood, some spoke a last 'good-bye',
'Ere they charged the Huns, mid the crash of guns, on the 1st day of July.

O'er shell ploughed ground with barbed wire strewn, the storm of steel did sweep,
The Bosche defences stayed them not, into their trench they lead;
Came into grips, came face to face, with the coward, wily, Hun,
Who with wild alarms, throw down their arms, crying 'Kamarade' they run.

The first trench taken, on again none faltering in the task:
The fourth is the objective that reached, 'twas all was asked:
'Forward' and 'No Surrender' ancient Derry's watch-word rang,
As on again the stormers came, not heeding cannon's bang.

The khaki line though thinning fast, unflinching forward goes.
Grappling with bomb and bayonet, the lurking hidden foes.
The still tenacious spirit of ancient Ulster's there.
Till task be done, till fourth line's won, the carnage they will bear.

The sun is sinking in the west, the shades of evening come;
Night falls upon the battle field of so much dared and done.
The '36th' in honour great have borne their gallant part,
The work they've willed has been fulfilled, with noble soldier heart.

Roll call revealed the names gone down, who fell in noble strife;
For freedom's cause and justice had made sacrifice of life;
For England's honour, Ulster's fame, they boldly dare and die.
In a soldier's grave, far across the wave from the land they love they lie.
ONE OF THE ELEVENTH

Now began the sad and tedious task of sorting out kit. Labelling it for return to stores and where possible ensuring that all personal items eventually got home to the soldier's family.

On July 4th the Eleventh were resting at Hedauville along with the remnants of 109 Bde. They were paraded in a football field. General Nugent spoke to them. Afterwards the Brigade Commander Brigadier-General R. Shuter addressed them. Finally the Eleventh were de-briefed by the Commanding Officer. At midday it began to rain heavily making the situation more sombre.

July 5th saw the Eleventh marching again and they arrived at Herissart shortly before six o'clock that evening. During the next few days everyone was employed in sorting out kits and in all the other routine work so poignantly necessary after the battle.

Orders were received on July 7th to be ready to move at one hour's notice. The only kit to be taken was as per mobilisation tables. This appears to convey that some emergency situation was anticipated. This state of readiness was not relaxed for the next two days and routine work continued under these conditions.

Continual re-location was part of the way of life for the next couple of weeks. First the Eleventh moved to Fieuvillers which they had marched through late in the previous November. This was a long march of over nineteen hours duration and they arrived at two o'clock on a warm and misty morning.

Next afternoon July 11th saw another march to Conteville. This took about four hours and then they boarded a train for Berguette arriving in the afternoon of July 12th after two o'clock.

This did not finish the weary journey of these men who had survived the world's most terrible battle just ten days ago. Exhausted but with good humour they marched for another six hours to billets in Racquingham.

Undaunted - shortly after ten next morning another march to Setques began. They arrived shortly before five o'clock in time for tea!

At last a respite was gained from all this tedious marching. The Eleventh remained at Setques for the next seven days.

In true Inniskilling fashion they began by cleaning the billets and the surrounding area. Ordinary training continued and a small draft of officers arrived including Capt. J.E. Knott D.S.O., Capt. F.C. Mountray, 2nd. Lt.d. A.G.F. Bell, J. Curley, J.A. Johnston and H. Malseed.

Another ten hour march began on July 21st when the Eleventh moved to Bollezeele marching through Quelmes, Moulle and Watler on a dusty road.

The next move the Eleventh made was in the luxury of buses and lorries. Leaving Bollezeele in the early afternoon of July 23rd they arrived at Romarin in the evening shortly after seven o'clock. They then marched to Red Lodge area in the Bois De Ploegsteert and relieved the 9th Royal Irish Fusiliers in reserve of 108 Brigade.

Apart from some gas alarms the area was quiet. Another draft of junior officers arrived namely J. Robertson, W.E. Hewitt, T.H. Bowen, E. Wilkinson, J.F. O'Brien and C.W. Fawkes.

The Eleventh remained in reserve until July 28th when, following another gas alarm, they relieved the 11 R. West Kents in the trenches from Ploegsteert to Messines Road. This included Douve and eight bays of Winter Trench. Battalion Headquarters remained at Hill 63. A platoon of each company with thirty-five men plus the Lewis Gun teams held these trenches. It took about three hours to complete the relief which was finalised early next morning.

Later that day a small draft arrived consisting of 2nd Lt. C.H. McComb and five men.

The situation remained quiet and on the last day of July the Eleventh mustered thirty-eight Officers and four hundred and seventeen other ranks. So ended the month of July for the Eleventh Inniskillings. It had been their hard fortune to help bear the brunt of the fighting in the left sector of the attack on July 1st. This sector had been impregnable. The attack on the left although gaining little ground had at least helped the attack on the right.

The losses of that fateful morning brought mourning to many of their homes. The writer recalls seeing the relatives of the fallen wearing a sprig of the little blue forget-me-not as a memorial token on July 1st.

The situation remained quiet and on the last day of July the Eleventh mustered thirty-eight Officers and four hundred and seventeen other ranks.

CHAPTER 16

Distinguished Service

The Eleventh were in the trenches at Ploegsteert Wood on the first day of August. "Plugstreet" to every soldier in the army.

The month had a familiar beginning because Capt. F. C. Moutray and Pte P. Craven of C Coy were wounded by shrapnel from Artillery fire.

The usual routine of relief took place and while D Coy remained in reserve at Hill 63 the rest of the Battalion went back to rest billets at Romarin.

There was a small draft of eight men from base. The main activity being training specialists and providing working parties.

The need for more recruits was very great so Capt. Crosbie and several soldiers went back to Ireland for this purpose.

At the same time a substantial draft of ninety men and 2nd Lt. J. Kennedy were attached from the Sherwood Foresters, The Notts. and Derby Regiment.

The acute shortage of officers is made apparent by the fact that Capt. Moore took command of the Battalion when Lt. Col. Brush went on leave.

A composite company held the front line trenches in the second week of August under Capt. Knott DSO. Another composite company commanded by Lt. B. F. McCorkell was in reserve with Battalion headquarters under Capt G. M. Forde at Hill 63.

L / Cpl. J. Doherty and L / Cpl McKay and 2 Lt. A. G. Bell were wounded by shell fire.

The King paid a visit to Second Army area on August 14th. The high note of this visit was that Lt. H. Gallaugher and Pte W. J. Fleming were presented to him.

Later W. J. Fleming reached the rank of Corporal. He was the son of Hugh and Anna Fleming of Tattykeeran. He died at home in June 1918 from meningitis as a result of gas poisoning and was buried in Colebrooke Churchyard. He was a member of Colebrooke Hanover L.O.L. 215.

Lt. H. Gallaugher had been commissioned from Sergeant on 23rd January 1915.

On August 20th notification was received by the Eleventh that Lt. H. Gallaugher had been awarded the Distinguished Service Order for conspicuous gallantry on July 1st and afterwards. The citation in the London Gazette of 22nd September 1916 says:
"For conspicuous gallantry in action. When other officers became casualties he took command and led on his men with great dash. Seeing the enemy firing on our wounded, he got into a shell hole with a private, and shot six enemy snipers with a rifle. Finally, he volunteered and with 20 men rescued 28 wounded men under very heavy fire."
The Crucifix, Thiepval, 1st July 1916, and Martinsart Wood 3rd/4th July 1916

This award really delighted everyone because Lt. Henry Gallaugher was a very popular officer.
On the same day came the news that Sgt. J. A. Hunter had been awarded the Distinguished Conduct Medal for conspicuous gallantry on July 1st.

He joined a platoon of another Battalion and got to the enemy's front line with only four men but held his own for eight hours as long as his bombs lasted. He rushed and knocked out a machine-gun taking seven prisoners. He chased two enemy officers who were finally captured by some men of another regiment.

The war was dragging on now and the battle of the Somme would continue to the end of September.

Almost two years previously Sgt. Wylie of the North Irish Horse had written home following the battle of the Marne. He remarked that he was glad to see how the Volunteers were doing but thought that they would not be needed as the Germans were on their last legs.

The experience of fellow countrymen now showed how wrong his assessment proved to be.

The men were living in the open air and all had large appetites. The feeding arrangements were rightly generous. Each man had daily one and a quarter pounds of bread or a pound of biscuit, four ounces of bacon, three ounces of cheese and four ounces of jam.

In addition there were three ounces of jam, a few spoonfuls of tea and eight ounces of vegetables. There was only two ounces of butter weekly and the soldiers had to get their heat energy from the liberal ration of jam and sugar.

These were the provisioning arrangements but there were times of hardship when supplies did not reach the trenches owing to enemy action.

These conditions are reflected in the determination and gallantry of C.Q.M.S. John Woods from Ballinamallard. On three different occasions he was in charge of pack transport which became disorganised under heavy shell fire. He collected his animals and led them to the dump.

Another time his was the only company to get food for two days. He also delivered the whole of the Battalion's rations under heavy shell fire in very difficult circumstances. He was later awarded the Distinguished Conduct Medal.

On August 20th Major A. C. Pratt 9th Royal Irish Fusiliers joined the Eleventh and took over Command from Capt. W. Moore.

At this time when not in the line the Battalion was providing working parties and under going specialist training whilst in Divisional reserve.

As is usual with all new Commanding Officers Major Pratt inspected the Battalion on joining. This was on August 21st prior to relieving the 9th Inniskillings in the trenches. A chance for the men to critically assess their new leader. The Eleventh remained in the trenches longer than usual and were not relieved until August 28th.

During this spell the usual rotation of companies in the front line was repeated. All the soldiers were well used to the routine of being on sentry or part of a patrol by now. The experience of sleeping in a dug out and the cold dawn stand to was now second nature to them all.

Divine service was arranged for C Coy and Battalion headquarters as the situation permitted it on Sunday August 27th at Hill 63.

Only one man was wounded in this period. He was Pte J. Thompson.

The Eleventh went in to Divisional reserve again following their relief by the 9th Inniskillings. A Coy remained at Hill 63. The remainder were in rest billets again at Romarin.

There were some opportunities for bathing and resting as the month drew to its close.

CHAPTER 17

Knobkerries by Moonlight

Following a church service on Sunday September 3rd the Eleventh relieved their comrades of the 9th Inniskillings. This was a system with which these two Battalions were now very familiar. The Donegals and Tyrones trading banter and bits of information as they did so.

The good humour and droll wit of these countrymen from the west of Ulster punctuated the official military exchanges as they swapped positions. The tasks of checking equipment, indicating arcs of fire and telling ranges were coloured by the homely phrases of the farms and the workplaces they often thought of.

The relief was completed well after ten o'clock when a Brigade order was received. This stated that the Eleventh would remain in the line for three days and then move to a new sector.

The Eleventh remained here at Pleogsteert Wood without incident until relieved by the 10th Worcesters. Headquarters with A and D Coys went back to rest billets at Romarin. The remainder stayed in reserve at Stirling Castle.

More marching had to be endured. On September 7th when the Eleventh marching to their band moved to a new Brigade area at Dranoutre. This took over four and a half hours and they arrived at their new position after five o'clock to find themselves in Brigade reserve. The severe shortage of officers was ameliorated to some degree by the arrival of Lts. W. A. Murphy, A. H. Muir, J. Scott and 2nd Lt. T. C. Sweeney.

Lt. Murphy had been a chemist in Enniskillen before the war.

In this second week of September the men from the Sherwood Foresters who were attached transferred and were given Inniskilling numbers.

Several men were wounded by artillery fire. L/Cpl R. Megahey was awarded the Military Medal.

Notification was also received of the award of the M.C. to C.S.M. Bullock. The citation for Bullock's Millitary Cross gives some measure of the man and his determination:

"When all his officers became casualties he led the company on most gallantly and consolidated in the enemies' third line. Though wounded, he stuck to his post. When forced to retire he was cut off while covering the retirement and taken prisoner, but he fought his way through with his fists being again severely wounded, and rejoined his Battalion."

Happily he survived the war. During the Second World War he served in the U.S.C. with some distinction.

Major Pratt - who had served in the South African War and had been mentioned in Despatches - was soon to be promoted to Lt Col. He decided to make a raid on the enemy positions. He wanted intelligence to determine if gas was installed in the enemy position, the name of the enemy unit and the positions of machine-guns.

The raid - which was meticulously planned - was to be carried out by four raiding parties divided into small groups of men. Each group was led by an N.C.O. In overall command was 2nd. Lt. T. Adams. It was very well supported by the Artillery.

These men were all heavily armed with rifles, bayonets and knobkerries. They also carried ten bombs each and they had scaling ladders, wire cutters, grapnels and amongst other equipment a dinner bell for signal purposes.

They left their own trenches at the south corner of the Bull Ring to enter the enemy trenches forty five yards east from their own position on the night of September 15th.

As they went over the parapet they heard cheers from a neighbouring trench, "Go on the Inniskillings". It turned out that the cheers came from the Enniskillen Nationalist Volunteers in the "Irish Brigade', who gave a hearty-send off to their Orange brethren from the home county. Their trenches were on the immediate left of the Eleventh at that particular time.

They crossed their own parapet at a quarter to nine with the moon rising behind some cloud. They formed up in a large shell crater twenty-five yards from their own trench. Dashing forward they entered the enemy position through an unbelievably convenient gap in the wire.

A sentry challenged them as the leaders were mounting the parapet, fired a couple of shots and missed. Stray bullets from machine-gun cross fire in No Man's Land caused two casualties.

The first group led by L/Cpl Charles Wray from Taughboyne, Co. Donegal went south along the enemy front line. They met tough resistance and retaliated with bomb and bayonet. They killed eight and took one prisoner. A deep dug out was bombed. Sets of equipment were found on the parapet and these were thrown out but could not be recovered later.

L/Cpl Wray having used all his bombs collected German grenades and used them very effectively.

Sadly he was killed in this raid. He was awarded the M.M. for his courage on July 1st but the notification was not published until 4th October 1916. He did not live to receive his award.

Led by Sgt O'Hara the second group initially passed the communication trench they were to bomb and block. Having found it and done good work they were then bombed by the enemy from their second line. L/Cpl Fern led a small party and successfully bombed the second line.

Pte Orgill skilfully bombed a dug out from which loud screams and shouts were heard.

L/Cpl Alex McKay was killed while energetically engaging a group of the opposition's bayonet men.

Then the enemy collected in a large number but with accurate bombing and revolver fire twenty of them were killed or wounded.

The third group led by L/Cpl Donaldson chased a group of Germans down the first line trench. Donaldson had a Mills bomb in his hand with the pin in. He struck a German on the head with it and then killed him with his knobkerrie.

No gas cylinders or machine-gun positions were found. Three men were slightly wounded.

The other groups bombed the enemy positions as planned and had several men slightly wounded in the process.

One prisoner was brought in and some documents were found. No gas or machine-guns were found and it was learned the enemy wire was in poor condition with gaps in some places. Some mining operations were seen.

The N.C.O.s in command of each small group had displayed very capable leadership and this was later commended by the C.O. 2nd Lt. Thomas Adams was awarded the M.C. "For conspicuous gallantry when leading a raid. He entered the enemy's trenches. It was largely due to his skill and determination that the raid was successful."

He was popularly known as 'Tiny' Adams because of his great stature and strength.

Following the raid the German lines were heavily shelled by the Artillery which did enormous damage. Sgt. J. Wright Ptes, J. Binks and G. Routledge were wounded by a Canadian trench mortar bomb which was prematurely fused. The Canadians were on the immediate left of the Eleventh.

Sgt J. O'Hara, L/Cpl H. Fern and Pte J. McConnell were awarded the M.M. Ptes Orgill and Dodwell were commended for their good work. Following the success the remainder of the month saw several small actions and a number of men were wounded. Sgt. J. Hunter received the medal of St. George third class.

On one afternoon the Battalion went to the cinema at Bailleul. Afterwards they were given two hours to visit the town. A draft of sixty-seven men arrived and they were welcomed as an essential addition to the fighting strength.

The Battalion Orange Lodge The Inniskillings True Blues No. 870 met as often as they possibly could. After the transaction of the business a social hour was held, as if they were at home, and at this the officers were present, including Bros. Major C. F. Falls and Lieutenants Gordon and Knight. Bro. Halliday was the Master of the lodge, and Bro. Lewis was the Deputy Master.

The Battalion moved to rest billets at Aircraft Farm on the last day of September.

Working parties still had to be found for all the tasks which were so necessary to life in the war.

There were several routine reliefs in the line. Most of these were without incident except on October 9th when four men were wounded by shrapnel.

The official notification was received that R.S.M. Bleakley was awarded the M.C. for his gallant work on 1st July 1916.

A strong patrol went out on October 10th after a gas discharge but were unable to reach the enemy lines. No useful intelligence was gained from trying to operate in such difficult conditions.

Later in the month Pte. Clarke J.T. and Pte. Marriott G. were killed. This was the result of retaliatory fire during a raid by the 9th Inniskillings.

Another period was spent in Divisional Reserve. The usual recreation was organised as far as working routine permitted. The inter company football final was played with C and D Coy as the finalists. Result D Coy 3 goals C Coy 1 goal.

The cinema was visited once again in Bailleul and the men were entertained to tea in the town.

At the end of October the Eleventh were in Derry Camp in Brigade Reserve until they took over the 9th Inniskilling position. This was at Hallowe'en and the usual pranks and customs from their native counties were enacted as far as the situation permitted.

The traditional tasty items for this old country festival were in abundance courtesy of the Comforts Fund. Everyone was greatly heartened by these gifts from the thoughtful organisers at home. They conveyed the vital message that the men were not forgotten.

CHAPTER 18

At the Moon's Rise

More casualties heralded the start of this period. In bad weather the trenches had their share of incoming trench mortar and artillery fire. Eight were wounded and two killed including L/Cpl. John Walker of Enniskillen.

A practice Alarm revealed that the whole Battalion was ready to move in half an hour.

Another large raid took place on the enemy trenches. The aim being to find out details about tunnelling, machine-gun positions, gas installation and trolley lines. The planning and instructions for the raid are highlighted by their great detail and thoroughness.

The raid started in the early evening with the entry into the German trenches at a quarter to eight just at the rise of the moon on Tuesday November 14th.

A total of four officers and one hundred and eighty men took part. Collectively they were designated as 'G' Coy. This included specialists on tunnelling from the Sappers. The equipment carried was very comprehensive and included ammonal tubes, axes, bombs and Lewis guns. Everyone's faces were blackened with burnt cork. Steel helmets were worn and gas helmets carried.

There was no preceding artillery barrage but trench mortar fire was intensified for several days beforehand. A Box Barrage could be put down by a pre-arranged signal. Each company provided a party of men for the raid. The officers involved were 2nd. Lts. Strong, Johnston, Malseed and Talbot.

The men had been trained in No Man's Land in preparation for this particular raid. Training in the use of German hand grenades had also been completed as well as training in the use of the German machine-gun. Nothing was left to chance preparing for this raid. The careful organisation of the supply of Mills grenades had been perfected. The complexity of this raid made it vital for each man to be totally aware of what he had to do. They were organised in groups of three to five in each squad so everyone knew his comrades.

This extract from Lt. Col. Pratt's Operation's Order clearly shows the detailed planning and illustrates the heavy responsibility placed on each squad. The other three parties had similar orders.

RIGHT PARTY		Off.	N.C.O.	Men
No. 1 Squad.	Ammonal Tube Party	-	1	3
No. 2 Squad.	Right 1st Line Blocking Party.	-	1	4
	Search Party.	-	-	2
No. 3 Squad.	Back Communication Trench Blocking Party.			
	a. Trolley Line.	-	1	5
	Search Party.	-	-	2
	b. Right Back Communication Trench Blocking Party.	-	1	5
	c. Right 3rd Line Blocking Party.	-	1	5
	Search Party.	-	-	2
	Lewis Gun Party.	-	1	3
No. 4 Squad.	Right 2nd Line Blocking Party.	-	1	5
	Search Party (Dugout V)	-	-	2
No. 5 Squad.	Centre 2nd Line Blocking Party.	-	1	4
No. 6 Squad.	Pivot Party.	<u>1</u>	<u>1</u>	<u>4</u>
	TOTAL	1	9	46

The signalling arrangements included Very lights and parachute rockets. There were also torches covered in red paper for identification purposes. This was vitally necessary to prevent one party from bombing another.

Photographs taken from the air provided important intelligence for the planning of this raid. The raid was to be conducted in two phases.

The first phase would be the raid on the first, second and third line of the enemy trenches. The second phase would be on the fourth line and the signal to begin would be two green Very lights fired from our own position. Keeping strictly to the timing for the raid all four parties swiftly moved over the parapet. Headed by the ammonal tube group they crawled to the selected shell craters close to the enemy trench.

The first party from D. Coy, led by 2nd. Lt. Strong exploded the ammonal tube and rushed the German trench and killed any who resisted. Deadly dexterity with the bayonet was the hallmark of these raiders of the Eleventh.

Moving quickly up the main communication trench they met a group of enemy bombers. Killing four of the enemy they quickly blocked that part of the trench.

Another group from D Coy following the communication trench to the second line found it blocked with concertina wire. An enemy sniper fired and wounded one man. A grenade was thrown and the sniper was no more.

Going south the right second line party met stiff opposition but overcame it. They counted ten dead enemy and using bombs supplied by another group had a spirited contest when the enemy counter attacked.

Altogether this group used over six hundred bombs and accounted for thirty of the enemy. They also knocked out a machine-gun which was firing but could not reach it because the trench was very strongly wired.

There was no gas installed in the first or second line and the trenches were duck boarded and badly damaged by shell fire.

The C Coy group led by 2nd. Lt Johnston got off to a perilous start. The ammonal tube party were discovered as they were placing it in position and were bombed. There were two immediate casualties and disastrously the tube was bombed and exploded.

With determination and not a little courage they moved on as far as the second line. Here they found a large dug out which was an important objective just after they had killed a couple of snipers. They destroyed the dug out and killed a further seven of the enemy with a bag of ammonal.

Their inspection of the trenches revealed that no gas was installed and that they were badly damaged by shell fire. The second line had a broad trench which was four feet wide at the bottom and contained the trolley line with a two and a half foot gauge. This trench was six feet deep and ten feet wide at the top.

Finally the raiders could find no trench mortars, machine-guns or mining but they did take a wounded prisoner of 104 Saxon Regiment.

The third raiding party from B Coy were equally successful although they met tough resistance from bombers at the start. The left front line group had several casualties but they drove the enemy back and killed two of them. Demolishing a dug out - which was constructed from concrete a metre thick - the right second line group pushed on using their Lewis gun with deadly effect.

The enemy organised a counter attack which was demolished by eleven magazines from the Lewis gun. This weapon was invaluable according to the after battle report.

Two prisoners were captured - one who had been found at the bottom of a listening gallery. The other prisoner was a miner who appeared willing to give information and he was sent to Brigade Headquarters for interrogation. Detailed examination of the objective again revealed that no gas was installed and that the trenches were in poor condition. Signs were found of trolley lines completely smashed by shellfire.

The fourth party from A Company had a particularly unlucky start to their part in the raid. Early on they were spotted and bombed by the enemy. The ammonal tube would not explode despite heroic efforts to fire it. The tube and its firing team were put out of action by enemy bombs.

Hard pressed and being unable to gain an entrance to the enemy trenches a report was sent back to the Commanding Officer. He immediately ordered them to withdraw.

Overall this raid demonstrated the professionalism of the whole Battalion in its planning and execution. The length of the line raided was almost three hundred yards and the depth took in the enemy's first, second and third lines.

For good work and gallantry in this raid 2nd. Lt. Strong was awarded the Military Cross. The citation says "For conspicuous gallantry in action. He led a raiding party against the enemy's trenches with great gallantry, blew up a mine shaft, captured three prisoners, and accounted for over thirty of the enemy. He has on many previous occasions done fine work".

Sgt. Robert Roulston from Newtowncunningham was awarded the Divisional Certificate for his coolness and accuracy in bombing.

There were fourteen men wounded, one man missing and one killed during the raid. The outcome was very useful and included maps, documents, three prisoners taken and proof no gas was installed. Sixty of the enemy had been killed excluding those accounted for by the Box Barrage.

There were many congratulatory messages following the raid. The Army Commander in particular referred to the valuable information obtained and the damage inflicted on the enemy. The raiders had brought much honour to themselves and the regiment.

R.S.M. Bleakley M.C. who was married to an Enniskillen lady had a short spell of leave. At home in Halesowen a civic reception was held for him. He and Mrs. Bleakley were driven through the town led by the town band in a procession which included the police, a detachment of the Devonshire Regiment and many others.

Prior to going on leave he had been shaving in his dugout when a shell burst nearby lifting him clear out of the dugout but miraculously he was unharmed.

His citation for the Military Cross says:
"For conspicuous gallantry in action. Though wounded he refused to go to hospital, and took part in the attack next day, when he was again wounded. On the evening of that day he rallied, and sent back to their units men who were getting out of hand. Later, when retirement was ordered, he got together enough men to form a line to repulse any attack the enemy might make."

After this raid - which had raised the morale of everyone very considerably - life continued in the line. There were more casualties particularly from a violent bombardment on November 24th.

This letter written by the Chaplain poignantly reveals the caring duty they had to perform and the sad circumstances in which it was written. The work of the Chaplains was continuous. A great deal was expected of them and they were selfless in their devotion to all.

11th Royal Inniskilling Fusiliers,
B.E.F., France,
25th Nov. 1916.

Dear Mrs. Bowes,
    It is my painful duty to send you news which cannot but cause you a very great shock, concerning your son Lce. Cpl. J. Bowes, No. 16833 of this Battalion. Late last night the part of the line in which your son's Company is placed, was heavily bombarded by the German trench-mortar batteries. I regret very much to say that one of these shells fell into the midst of the party of men of which your son was one, and he and another man were instantaneously killed.
    He did not suffer a moment, but died at once without speaking or moving. The force of these great explosives is so powerful that all sensa-

tion is suspended and death comes perfectly painlessly. I hope it may be a little comfort to you to know that your boy did not suffer.

I realise that even with this little consolation what I have written must come as a dreadful shock to you, but the truth must be told no matter how hard it is to bear. I hope and pray that God will be very near you now when you need His help. Do not fail to ask Him to be with you now.

I believe your husband is dead; so it will need all your courage to face your future without your eldest son to help you.

May God bless you! Yours very sincerely,
Alexander Spence,
Chaplain.

The Communion set of the Rev. Spence is on display in the Regimental Museum.

A couple of days later 2nd. Lt. Strong led a patrol to the German lines. A letter written by one of the prisoners captured in the recent raid was left with a notice saying that if any of the enemy surrendered they would be well treated.

The Eleventh remained in the Ploegsteert area for the next month. There were several marches to relieve other units as the need arose. There was another march to Kortepyp where they were inspected by Sir Douglas Haig. Commander in Chief on December 20th.

On Christmas Day 1916 there was Artillery activity on both sides during the morning. The companies carried out inter company relief. Half of A and D Coys in the front line. The other half being in Half Way House. B Coy was in the subsidiary line and C Coy at Hyde Park Corner.

There was some opportunity to enjoy festive fare and local celebrations were observed.

Cpl David Barnhill from Ballylawn Co. Donegal and Sgt. Bleakley were posthumously awarded the M.M. for bravery in the field during the beginning of 1916. Pte. H. McCartney also received the M.M. in similar circumstances.

So ended the long hard year for the men of Donegal and Fermanagh.

CHAPTER 19
Another Year

The main Christmas activities were held on New Year's Day. There was a festive start to another year and everyone enjoyed the break.

To add further to morale it was learned that Lt Col Pratt had been awarded the D.S.O. Capt Crosbie the Medical Officer and Capt Myles were awarded the M.C. The Battalion spent the remainder of the month in the line in very severe frost.

February began by seeing the Eleventh in Brigade Reserve. The hard frost continued. There were many working parties and several reliefs were provided to the Derrys. This lively letter says it all.

Dear Sir,
    I have great pleasure in acknowledging your kind and welcome parcel of the old favourite Woodbines which I received in the trenches. We are enjoying a very comfortable smoke in our dug-out. The warm soup which we get every night has just gone round, and the boys are just singing Keep the Home Fires Burning as I am writing these few lines to you.

    The weather this last while has been very severe with the frost and snow, but the boys from the old town all keep smiling. All we are short of at present is a mouth organ to cheer our neighbours across the way, as they are very downhearted, as his old coal boxes are nearly all duds, but once our flying pigs goes over he has to take to his heels. I now thank you again for the Woodbines, as all the boys say that there is none to beat the ones from the old Skin town. - From some of the old reliables of A Company, 11th Battalion, Royal Inniskilling Fusiliers. - Signed, yours faithfully,

                    14091 Sgt. McClintock, R. J.
                    17962 Cpl. Hamilton, W. D.
                    14120 Cpl. Simpson, P.
                    17283 L. Cpl. Elliott, W. R.

In February Mr. Alan Osborne a solicitor in Milford, Co. Donegal received this correspondence from Mrs. Hessey. This shows the widespread support for the Comforts Fund and the use to which it was put.

Bramham Gardens, London, S.W., January, 1917.

Dear Mr. Osborne - I am enclosing you a memorandum which will show you how the 11th Inniskillings Comforts Fund stands at present, as far as the general account is concerned.

As agreed upon with you and the other members of committee, we have arranged to pay a quarterly subscription of £40 to the Battalion Fund, to be used by the Commanding Officer on the spot at his discretion for comforts, etc.

I have had a most grateful letter from Colonel Pratt telling me what a great benefit our first contribution has been to the men. He has spent a certain amount of the money on supplementing the potato ration and on buying green vegetables, &c.

You will notice that the officers' subscription to this fund for the past year amounted to £223 14s 9d, so that in reality we are only returning part of this money to be spent by the Battalion locally, and are not using any county contributions for this purpose.

With the regards to the prisoners, it has been decided by the Central Committee Prisoners of War that each prisoner must receive three parcels of food fortnightly. In the case of the 11th Inniskillings this Comforts Fund pays for one parcel, Lady Carson's Fund pays for another, and a third is sent by a friend or adopter in connection with the Ulster Womens' Gift Fund.

As at present the 11th prisoners number only three, the expense incurred under this heading is small, but, of course, we must keep a considerable sum of money set aside for future possible needs.

We send out a good number of newspapers weekly, also games, &c., and I am arranging, at the request of the chaplain, to send out books for the men.

Our last Christmas present took the form of fruit for the Christmas Day dinner, oranges, apples, sweets, nuts &c.

With regard to woollen comforts, we are not making any appeal, as the Government supplies seem quite adequate now, but we are forwarding any parcels that are sent to us, and socks are always welcomed by the men, as the handmade socks are, of course, very superior to what they get from the ordnance.

I hope that you will let me know if you have any further suggestions to make with regard to the working of this fund, as we are most anxious to carry out the wishes of the subscribers.

    Yours sincerely,
    P. HESSEY
    Hon. Sec. 11th Inniskilling Comforts Fund

Army and Navy Club, Pall Mall, S.W., 1st February, 1917

Dear Mrs. Hessey,

Would you please convey to the committee and to the many subscribers to the Inniskillings Comforts Fund the very sincere thanks of all ranks of the Battalion for their generous gifts in money and in comforts to us. The money I have used for buying various "extras," which have gone to supplement the excellent rations given us by the authorities.

Yours very truly,

    A.C. PRATT, Lieutenant Colonel, Commanding 11th Batt. Royal Inniskillings Fusiliers.

In March the Eleventh went in to Divisional reserve. The weather was foul and training continued.

There was some marching despite the very bad weather. In one snow storm seven men had to fall out of the ranks.

Organised bathing arrangements helped to keep personal hygiene adequate and in the Brigade sports finals the Eleventh acquitted themselves well. B Coy under the command of Capt. Henry Gallaugher D.S.O. won the Brigade Rifle Championship. The Gallaugher sisters treasure the handsome silver flask trophy to this day. It was presented by Brigadier General Ricardo.

6 Platoon won the Lewis Gun Championship and the Bayonet Fighting Championship.

Pte G. Holmes won the Featherweight Boxing Championship.

Such were the activities to develop interest and physical ability when in reserve and prepare for future action.

Through all the war Mr. W. Trimble of Enniskillen was a generous benefactor of the Eleventh and recently had sent out two cases of twenty thousand cigarettes each.

This nominal roll illustrates a platoon organisation and gives the names of the local Fermanagh men in it.

    Roll of No. 4 Platoon 11 Bn. R. Inniskilling Fusiliers 1917

C.Q.M.S. Brock, W. J.	
Sergt. Brabrooke, M.	Pte. Stirrip, J. H.
Sergt. Riley, R.	Pte. Evens, J.
Sergt. Armstrong, R.	Pte. Cadden, T.
Sergt. Bruce, G. H.	Pte. Humphrey, H.
Cpl. Noble	Pte. Noble, J.
Cpl. Edwards, J. R.	Pte. Saunders, G.
Cpl. Keys, W. R.	Pte. Teirnan, M.
Cpl. Irvine, R.	Pte. Dillon

Samuel Canning

UVF in Co. Donegal near St. Johnston. Early 1913.

Donegal Ulster Volunteers at Baronscourt, 1913.

The photograph which cost 3d.
Donegal UVF at Finner Camp. Robert Roulston in background right.
Shirt and trousers for good weather.

Manorcunningham
UVF, Finner Camp
1914.

Left to right: Robert
Porter, John Roulston,
Robert Roulston left
kneeling, Alex Glenn
right kneeling.

Fermanagh Volunteers, 2nd Battalion, at Derrybrusk.

Parade on Broad Meadow of 3rd Battalion UVF.

'A' Coy 11th (U.V.F.) Royal Inniskilling Fusiliers
Recruiting March - November 1914 (Irvinestown)
Sitting behind the band. Left to Right: Sgt Dundas; Sgt Devers; Sgt Master-Cook Cowan; Sgt Irvine; Sgt Creswell; Sgt Mjr Chambers; Lieut Moore; Lieut Falls; Capt Falls; Lieut Cavandish-Butler; Lieut H.C. Gordon; C.Q.M.S. Hestwayle; Clr Sgt Russell (Inst of Musketry) Essex Regt. Band of the 4th Battalion

Major The Earl of Leitrim, First Commanding Officer of the Eleventh. 1915.

Lord Lieutenants' Inspection of 11th Inniskillings at Randalstown. Picture shows Viceroy inspecting 'A' Company. Major Falls is at the right of his men on horseback.

The Officers of the 11th Bn The Royal Inniskilling Fusiliers at Bramshot 1915.

Back row: 2nd Lt. G.M.F. Irvine. Lt. B.F. McCorkell. Lt. W.H. Wagentreiber. 2nd-Lt. A.C. Hart. Lt. C.B. Falls. 2nd-Lt. W.R. Williamson. 2nd-Lt. H.C. Pallant.
Second Row: 2nd-Lt. J.D. McIldowie. 2nd-Lt. A.D.C. Browne. 2nd-Lt. R. Grant. 2nd-Lt. L.H.N. Rutledge. 2nd-Lt. L.O.M. Munn. Lt. R.G. Orr. Lt. D.E. Crosbie, R.A.M.C.
Lt. H.C. Gordon. Lt. G.H. Webb. 2nd-Lt. W.M. Knight.
Third Row: Lt. & Qm. Mr. J.W. Firth. Capt. G.M. Forde. Capt. H. Cavendish Butler. Capt. W. Moore. Maj. The Earl of Leitrim. Lt-Col. W.F. Hessey. Maj. C.F. Falls. Capt.
W.T. Sewell. Capt. J.S. Miles. Capt. F.G. Boyton. Capt. J. Ballantine.
Front Row: 2nd-Lt. J.R.M. Hanna. 2nd-Lt. J.A.T. Craig.

The Sergeants of the 11th Bn The Royal Inniskilling Fusiliers. R.S.M. Bleakley is on the right of Major The Earl of Leitrim. Bramshot 1915.

Stewart Buchanan, Burt. KIA 1st July 1916.

Pte. James Quigley, No.3 section, Machine-Gun Company. KIA 1.7.1916.

A heavy load to carry

A TREBLE SACRIFICE

Left: Pte. James Simpson, KIA 29.6.1916. Right: Pte. Robert Simpson who died in a hospital in England on 25th August 1915 of pneumonia.

Pte. Joseph Simpson, KIA 1.7.1916. All three served in 11th Royal Inniskillings and were the sons of Mr. & Mrs. T Simpson, Castlecoole, Enniskillen

Thiepval wood and remnants of machine gun post which fired on the 11th as they crossed the open ground.

Sunken Road where 11th crossed.

Sgt. T. Cairns M.M.

Rev A Spence MC Communion Set

Robert Roulston M.M. 11th Inniskillings.

Above: The wounded in hospital clothes. D. Donldson extreme right with crutch.
Left: Davy Donaldson
Below: A nursing sister who cared for D. Donaldson

AWARDED THE MILITARY CROSS

Captain Rev. Jackson Wright    Captain J. S. Myles

Waiting for the Casualities
Drawing in Author's possession

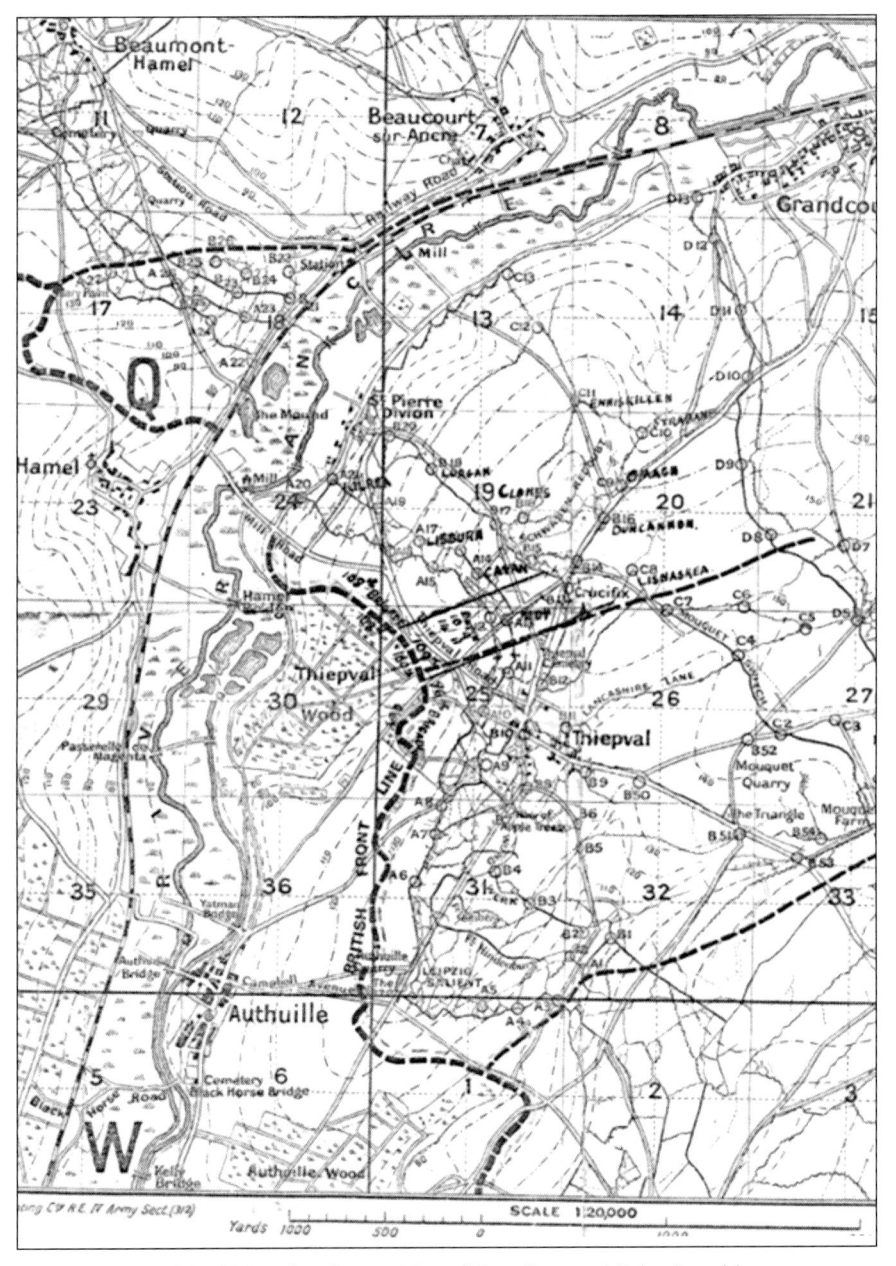

Original Map showing position of Battalions and Brigades with named objectives during attack.

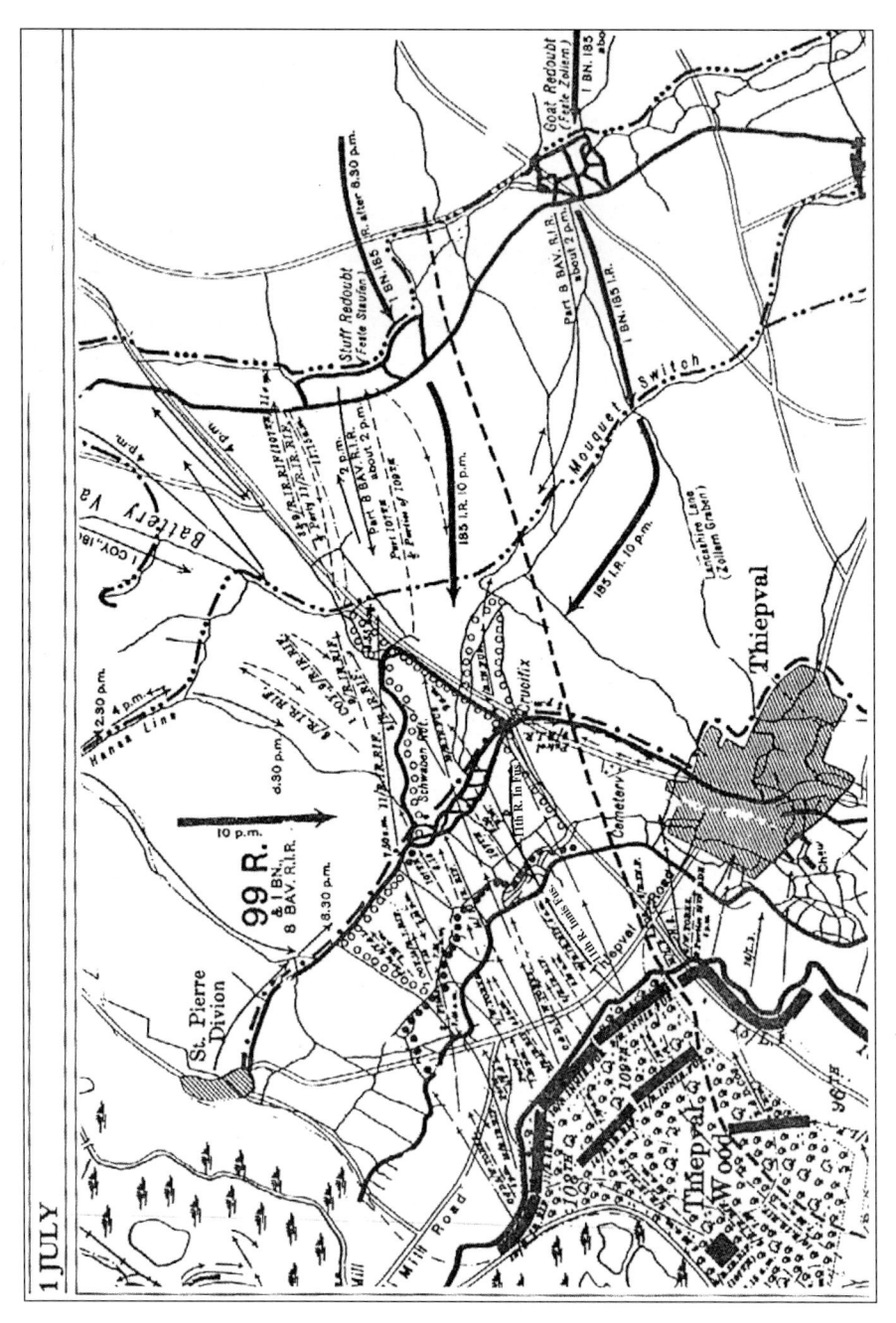

The Somme 1 July 1916 showing advance of Eleventh

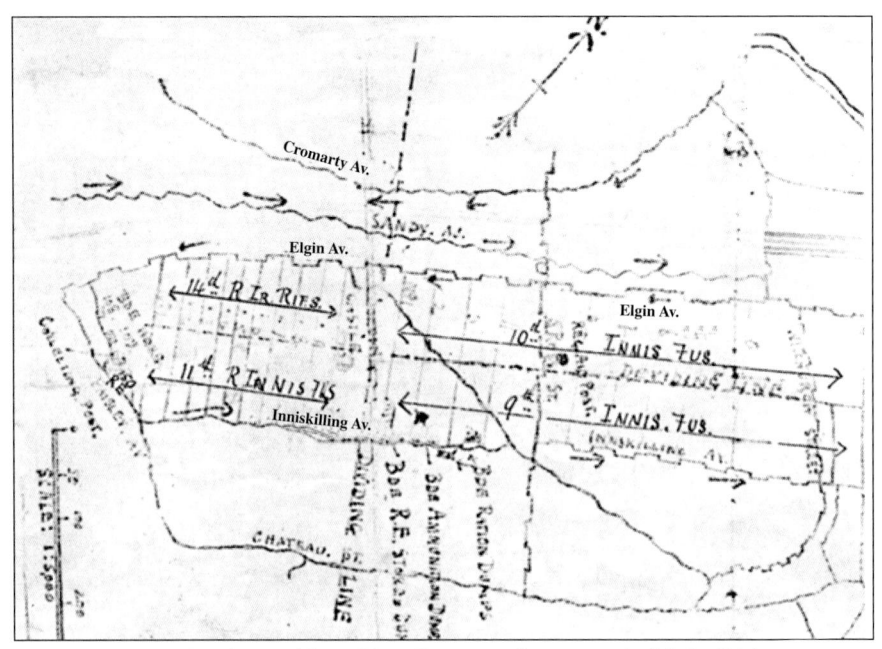

Map showing position of battalion preparing to attack. 1 July 1916

The British Offensive of 7 June against Messines Ridge, 1917

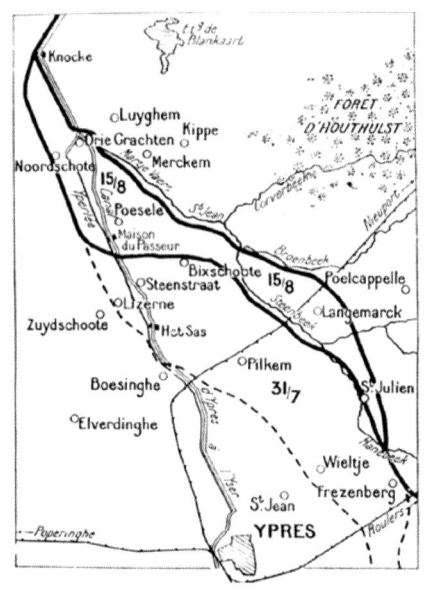

The Attack of 15 August 1917

ERECTED BY THE U.V.F.

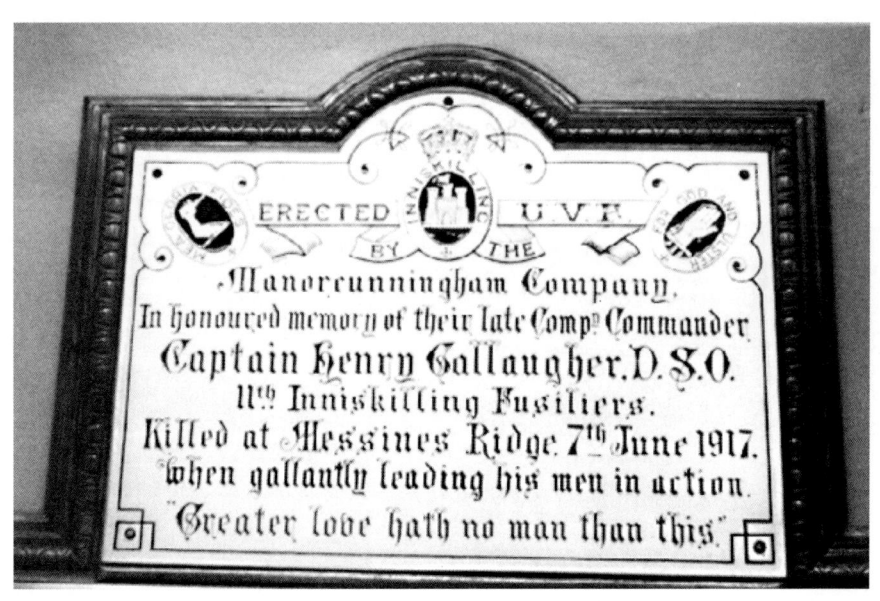

Manorcunningham Company.
In honoured memory of their late Comp? Commander
Captain Henry Gallaugher, D.S.O.
11th Inniskilling Fusiliers.
Killed at Messines Ridge 7th June 1917.
when gallantly leading his men in action.
"Greater love hath no man than this."

The memorial to Capt. Henry Gallaugher D.S.O.

Photo: Imperial War Museum

Officers of the Eleventh 12th June 1917.
This group includes Lt. Col. Pratt D.S.O. in the centre. He died of wounds 16th August 1917. Capt. Crosbie M.C. R.A.M.C. is standing on extreme right.

Photo: Imperial War Museum
The Eleventh advancing over German Line Nov. 1917

Photo: Imperial War Museum
The Eleventh in a captured trench Nov. 1917

Deserted Farm Houses, Cleenish,
originally provided for returning soldiers
Photos - Author

Captain J,W. Charlton M.C. & Bar who later
became County Surveyor Co. Fermanagh

John Stephenson,
Co. Donegal

Guy Bleakley M.C. with his youngest daughter and his
nephew Norris in 1932

J. Wallace third from left. Somme 50th Anniversary 1966.

G. Downey's grave in
Mill Rd. Cemetery
(Schwaben site) Lies flat
due to subsidence

Grave of Captain H.
Gallaugher D.S.O.
Lone Tree Cemetery

Grave of
W.T. McClintock,
Mill Rd. Cemetery

11th Battalion Colour   Donegal U.V.F. Colour

The Men of the Ulster Volunteer Force

The men of the Ulster Volunteer Force who assembled at Enniskillen on Sunday morning 8th December 1957 on the occasion of the laying-up of the Colours of the old Donegal U.V.F. Regiment in St. Macartin's Cathedral. The standard bearers are A. McMullan (on left) and J. McFarland. M.C. (right). Seated in the front row are, from left - James Irvine, James Lunny, David Brooks, Thompson Irvine, David McWilliam, Frank McConnell, Walter Hetherington, Thomas Weir; 2nd row - Henry Moffitt, J. Scott-Whyte, S. Bullock M.C., George B. Shields M.B.E., Irvine Pierce, W. B. Kells (directly behind Mr. Pierce), G. Parker, R. Humphreys, W. E. Trimble; back row - G. Breen, W. Clendinning, James Elliott, Thomas Foster, Adam Flanagan, William Maxwell, W. McCombes and Walter Quinn.

C.S.M. Bullock's Medals

C.S.M. Bullock M.C. 11th Bn., R. Innis. Fus.
taken in later years with U.S.C.

Louis Hazlett. D.C.M. M.M.

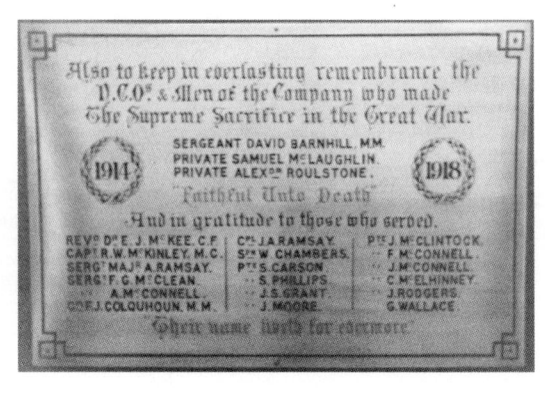

Top Left: Captured German Helmet Badge.

Top Right: A Memorial to the fallen and those who served in Ray Presbyterian Church Hall.

Left: Medals and Badges Sgt. Christopher Laird of Ballyshannon. K.I.A. 1 July 1916

The uniform & medals of Capt. J.W. Charlton M.C. and bar, Croix de Guerre.

Mrs. Mary Robb, widow of Pte H. Robb pictured on her 100th birthday March 27 1996, Bridgend, Co. Donegal

L/Cpl. McGahey, R.
L/Cpl. Scott, H.
Pte. Ditty, J. 13 sec.
Pte. Murphy, J.
Pte. Foster, W.
Pte. Prince, C.
Pte. Thompson, P.
Pte. Armstrong, F. S.
Pte. Crozier, F. G.
Pte. McGarrity, R.
Pte. Burke, J.
Pte. Booth, M.
Pte. Irvine, W.
Pte. Thompson, J.
Pte. Clarke, F.
Pte. Galtraith, J.
Pte. Tipping, J.
Pte. McIlfatrick

Pte. Drycott
L/Cpl. Hawkesworth, 14 sec.
Pte. Kichiney
Pte. Ryan
Pte. Simpson
Pte. Moore, T.
Pte. McDonagh, C.
Pte. Graham, J.
Pte. Leonard, J.
Pte. Cathcart, J.
Pte. Lowery, G.
L/Cpl. Armstrong
Pte. Little, G.
Pte. Ferris, W.
Pte. Hollahan, J.
Pte. Scott
Pte. Beattie, G. R.
Pt. McGrath

April begun with a snowstorm and a Church Service.

The Eleventh marched for two days in heavy snow to Hazelbrouck. The middle of April saw the Eleventh in the Spanbroek sector having spent nearly a week at Kemmel Hill. Working parties occupied nearly every hour but there were breaks for baths and company training. Having been relieved by the Derrys the Eleventh went to Brigade support at Kemmel. Ptes J. Richards and R. Mann were killed.

On April 29th the Artillery bombarded the enemy which resulted in aggressive retaliatory fire. From noon to tea time more than fifty shells landed in Kemmel village.

A number of men were awarded the Ulster Division Certificate for gallantry during the raids on enemy trenches including:
Sgt Major W. Lewis, Cpl T. Donaldson, Sgt H. White, L/Cpl T. Cairns and Pte. W. Gardiner.

Several officers who had shown an aptitude for flying or observing had on different occasions transferred to the Royal Flying Corps. Lt. D. P. F. Uniacke was accepted for observing duties and subsequently left at this time to take up his new appointment.

CHAPTER 20

Battle of Messines

The Eleventh were in the front line again in the Spanbroek left sector. There were several gas alarms but no gas was seen.

A large fire was seen behind the enemy trenches but the cause of it could not be determined.

Pte S. Toland from Tempo was killed at the beginning of the month of May.

On May 8th a dummy raid was carried out to induce the enemy to disclose their positions. The trench mortars shelled the enemy front line and support trenches. Then some dummy figures which had been positioned the night before were pulled up. Four enemy were seen running from the forward trench.

Everyone was now aware there was going to be another big battle. In one of his last letters to his mother Capt. Henry Gallaugher D.S.O. certainly gives a strong indication of a significant event being imminent.

Henry Gallaugher had already proved that he was an outstanding leader. His was a quiet and determined personality always willing to take on a hard task and see it through to the end.

From his strict but caring Presbyterian upbringing emerged a young man of vigour, prepared to do all he could for his men and to lead them by example. He also had a good sense of humour and a cheerful outlook on life.

He was educated at the Model School Londonderry and Moffats Private Academy in Letterkenny. He had been a company commander in the Ulster Volunteers in Manorcunningham.

His comments in all his correspondence, and in this particular letter, reveal a man prepared to lead from the front. This was not from any sense of foolish bravado but from a deep concern for those officers and men for whom he was responsible. A concern which cost him his young life. He was not remote from those he led and his attitude was one of sympathy and care.

For the next five days the Eleventh were resting, fitting out new clothing and

B.E.F.
19/5/17

My Dear Mother,
                Just a line to say
I am well, I am sure by the
time you get this you will have
seen Dr McKee as he goes on leave
in a day or two. I had a long talk
with the Colonel today & I must say
he does listen to reason, & he has
decided to let me go along with the
coy when going over the top
& I do trust it is for the best.
You see all the officers I have are
very young & inexperienced & it would
hardly be playing the game to
leave them, not saying that I can
do much more than they could, but
I have a little more experience & I
know the men a little better, besides
they have stood by me pretty well.
Just a little news, I understand that I have
been recommended for my majority & for the

the Legion of Honour. This of course I

equipment and cleaning up generally. They then went in to Divisional reserve. Headquarters was housed in Wakefield huts and the rifle companies in Kemmel Hill.

A couple of small drafts arrived and Lt. W. Follit and 2nd. Lt. C. W. Whiting went to the Indian Army.

The remainder of the month of May consisted of specialist training and the never ending work of shoring up trenches, keeping everything in good repair and preparing grenades.

On the last day of May the preliminary bombardment began.

Looking south from Plugstreet Wood Messines was a jumble of red roofs around an unattractive church and appeared to dominate the Flanders plain.

This position made it possible to carry out a major experiment in mining operations in an attempt to dislodge the enemy from his vantage point. The objective of General Sir Hubert Plumer's careful plan was to blow the Germans off the ridge.

The preparation for the attack was meticulous. Everything was thoroughly rehearsed on a model of the position.

Detailed Operational Orders were issued by Lt Col Pratt D.S.O.

He had to consider the ground over which the advance would take place. There was little cover. The enemy positions were very strong as he was aware of the attack and had time to prepare.

Previous German mining work had given them cause to believe from British tunnelling operations that something big was planned along their front. One example was an obstruction eighty feet down. They removed the timber and were staring into a huge mine chamber packed with thirty five tons of ammonal in tins. The German officer and eight men were killed trying to remove it.

Several other instances underground alerted the Germans but the white haired, precise and imperturbable Plumer had the exact date for the attack firmly decided.

In fact some of the local population were aware of the impending attack to the very day. A Belgium conscript had learned of it from girls in a cafe and it is believed they knew because they overheard some officers talking.

This Special Order of the Day was Issued

The Commanding Officer, on the eve of the Offensive, wishes to express thanks to every Officer, N.C.O. in which they have worked, willingly and whole-heartedly, in the interests of the Cause. He has the most thorough confidence that the Honour of their King and Country, and of the Regiment to which they have the honour to belong, will be upheld most honourably through all difficulties and dangers which may come in our way.

He wishes every Officer, N.C.O. and Man GOD SPEED and THE BEST OF LUCK as they go over the top.
(sgd.) A. C. Pratt, Lieut. Col.
Commanding 11th (S.) Battn. Royal Inniskilling Fusiliers

Emphasising the detail of the preparation there was one item which impressed the officers of the Inniskillings with its value. Every officer and N.C.O. had what was promptly named his "picture postcard". This was a card slip with a detailed map of the section of the enemy to be attacked. On the other side was a skeleton message with code signs to indicate important factors relating to the situation. With minimum effort this made it possible to mark down information and send it back as the attack developed.

The new system of organising the platoon into three sections - one for the Lewis gun one for bombers and one for rifle men - was used for the first time. Thus began the development of infantry fighting in small groups and would be refined as time went on to great effect.

Messines Ridge forms a shallow arc on the Flanders plain between Zillebeke and Ploegsteert. The chord of this arc, about nine miles long, was the site of the enemy front line system. Behind this, at the base of the arc, was the second line system. It would be wrong to write of a first trench, second trench and so on. Moving from front to rear of the position at least a score of trenches would be crossed.

Owing to this strength of the position it had to be taken at one go. There was four thousand yards of fortified country in between.

This whole honeycomb of trenches meant that stages of the attack were marked by defined lines on the map of the enemy position.

The Red line was the first stage drawn in front of the 36th and 16th Divisions on a map line just short of Wyteschaete Village. The second stage being the Blue line just beyond Wyteschaete Village. Stage three was the green line drawn to the edge of the road from Ypres to Messines. The fourth stage being the Black line drawn to the east of that road.

In the detail of his orders the Commanding Officer had to prepare for every eventuality.

It is only necessary here to cover those main points. On the right was B. Coy Commanded by Capt Henry Gallaugher D.S.O. forming the first wave. They had a platoon of 11th R.I.R. as moppers up. On the left C. Coy commanded by Capt W. Fluke with two platoons of 11th R.I.R. as moppers up. Support was provided by A Coy - Capt W. M. Knight and D. Coy Capt G. M. Forde M.C.

B and C Coys would lead the attack to the Red line at Naples Reserve which was the first objective. Then A and D Coys would leap frog through to the Blue line it being the second objective.

Here the 9th Inniskillings would leap frog through to the Black line on the far side of Wyteschaete.

The attack which was on a four platoon front in four waves had gone well from the start. Two strong points had to be constructed as soon as the Blue line was reached. Each platoon in the attack had carried four orange and green distinguishing flags attached to rifles.

At 2.30 a.m. the Eleventh formed up in the Assembly trenches.

Zero was 3.10 a.m. and mines exploded to the front. Peckham mine made a crater eighty yards in diameter and eighty feet deep.

The noise was so great it was heard in London. The sight defied description the flash and noise being unbelievable. There were huge smoke clouds of many colours and the earth shook.

Spanbroekmolen mine detonated fifteen seconds later. Many soldiers were killed by rubble and debris out in the open. They included men of the 16th and 36th Divisions.

Then the artillery barrage came down on the enemy lines. Twenty seconds after Zero the Eleventh deployed in to No Man's Land to attack. As the barrage lifted they were at the enemy's front line.

Almost immediately in the action Capt Henry Gallaugher D.S.O. was hit in the left arm. He continued to lead his men on characteristically saying "One of my wings is gone". His arm was shattered.

Refusing to go back he discarded the rifle which he could no longer carry. With great determination, his revolver in his right hand he went forward. "That's all right boys I'll do well with a revolver" he said. Just when the position was consolidated and secured he was killed by another shell.

The after battle report indicated that the artillery had been magnificent. By following up closely the infantry mopped up without serious opposition. The only difficulty was keeping the men from running in to the barrage as in many cases they were only thirty yards behind and fifty yards always proved a safe distance.

The Lewis gunners and rifle bombers dealt briskly with the enemy machineguns. One enemy machine gunner was found chained to his gun. The chain was broken by a rifle shot and this is the only instance the Eleventh found of a man being chained to his gun.

Tanks - which were a recent new addition to the battlefield - were unable to reach the Eleventh before they got to their objective nor was their help required.

Contact aeroplanes flew over the position indicated successfully by flares.
The message cards previously mentioned were used extensively in sending back information. Two messages were sent by pigeon. Within the hour of entering the enemy lines telephone messages were sent back.

The orders for reorganisation and all round defence placed great emphasis on the importance of having a strong wire entanglement in position prior to digging.

From all this the Eleventh contributed very significantly to the Intelligence picture at the rear headquarters.

At seven in the morning the villages of Messines and Wyteschaete were in British hands.

The result left the enemy completely devastated. An after battle report said that on the following day the battlefield was littered with bodies and debris. Some were half buried and others flattened. Wyteschaete was in ruins.

It was at Wyteschaete that Capt William Knight and his men had a very hot battle. At one time he was leading two companies because of casualties among the officers.

For his leadership he was awarded the M.C. The citation reads:

> "For conspicuous gallantry and devotion to duty. He commanded two companies during an attack, keeping them well in hand, and by his fine example and skilful leadership gaining the confidence of all the men in his vicinity. His orders were clear and complete, both for the attack and for the subsequent consolidation of the captured position. To his company belongs the credit of the capture of two enemy machine-guns and a field-gun."

He later won a bar to his M.C. and survived to become a successful lawyer and was registrar in the High Court in Belfast. Before the war he had been a young solicitor in Lisnaskea.

Notably in the battle there were four other Inniskilling Battalions. The 9th and 10th in 109 Brigade and the 7th and 8th with the 16th Division. Usually the former was known as the Inniskilling Brigade.

On the Blue line was a strong point known as Unnamed Wood. In recognition of the gallant part in its seizure by the Inniskillings it was officially designated Inniskilling Wood.

Thus ended the Battle of Messines.

The Eleventh moved back to the vicinity of Young Street and rested.

Next day June 9th they marched back to Wakefield Huts and occupied tents and bivouacs. They remained here for a few days and it was learned that C.S.M. Laird had been awarded the Medaille Militaire.

On June 13th some of the Battalion were working with 1st Canadian Tunnelling Coy. Headquarters and Transport moved to Mont Noir.

The Eleventh relieved the 10 R. Warwicks and 8th Glosters at Oosttaverne left sub sector and stores and transport were located at Lost Farm.

Having spent the remainder of the month in this area digging new trenches and providing working parties on June 30th they moved to Strazeele. The weather was poor and there were heavy showers.

The Eleventh mourned the loss of their beloved hero Capt. Henry Gallaugher D.S.O. For his gallantry at Messines he was recommended posthumously for the V.C. Unfortunately this was not to be and he received a posthumous Mention in Despatches. He had previously been mentioned in Despatches on 13th November 1916.

It is fitting that this chapter should end with these tributes to him which so eloquently express the character of the man.

109th Infantry Brigade.   36th (Ulster) Division.
IXth. Corps.   Date of Recommendation: 13th June 1917.

Unit: 11th (S) Battn. Royal Inniskilling Fusiliers.

Rank and
Name: Captain Henry GALLAUGHER, D.S.O.

Action for which commended:

On the 7th June 1917 in the SPANBROEK Sector on the occasion of the general attack on the MESSINES-WYTESCHAETE Ridge. This Officer was severely wounded before he reached the enemy first line, his left arm being broken. He threw down the rifle which he was carrying - slung on his left shoulder and said "That's all right boys I'll do well with a revolver." He continued to lead his men in the attack, stopping them when they got too close to our artillery barrage and giving his commands as cooly as if on parade and as if he had never been wounded. He led them to their final objective but just as his position which he had gained, was being consolidated, he fell, mortally wounded. His bravery has never been in doubt, he was the idol of his men and of the Battalion in general, and wherever he led his men would follow. His example on all occasions and on this day in particular remain an example which will always be treasured in this Battalion.

Recommended by: (Sgd.) A.C. Pratt, Lieut. Col.
                  Comdg. 11th (S.) Battn. R1. Inniskilling Fus.
Honour or Award: V.C.

11TH (S.) BATT. ROYAL INNISKILLING FUSILIERS
SPECIAL ORDER OF THE DAY

The Commanding Officer desires to place on record his appreciation of the manner in which the attack on the Enemy's position at WYTESCHAETE was carried out on the 7th inst. and the many deeds of gallantry that were performed, the result of which was that the Battalion carried each objective ordered, and consolidated the position taken, with the added result of nearly 200 prisoners, 2 machine-guns and 1 Field Gun.

The Commander-in-Chief, who viewed the operations, has already expressed his commendation of the work done by the Division in the attack.

While deploring the loss of our gallant comrades who have fallen in the fight, he feels convinced that the noble example of self-sacrifice set by such as Captain H. GALLAUGHER, D.S.O. who, although severely wounded, continued to fight on, will set us all an example of how a true Soldier can meet his death fighting for his King and Country and adding fresh honour to the laurels already won by this Battalion. His life and gallant end is an example until this War is satisfactorily concluded.

    (Sgd.) A.C. Pratt, Lieut. Col.
      Commanding 11th (S.) Battn. Royal Inniskilling Fusiliers.
IN THE FIELD
    8th June, 1917.

This tribute appeared in a local paper a few days later.

A BRAVE ULSTER OFFICER
Captain H. Gallaugher, D.S.O. Killed

Captain Henry Gallaugher, D.S.O., Royal Inniskilling Fusiliers, who has been killed in action in France, was the second son of Mr. John Gallaugher, Balleighan, Manorcunningham. He won the D.S.O. for his bravery in the big push in which the Ulster Division won glory on the 1st July, 1916. At that time he spent three nights in No Man's Land searching for the body of a brother Officer, a Derryman to whom he was much attached. In a special order of the day the Commanding Officer of the Battalion says: "While deploring the loss of our gallant comrades who have fallen in the fight the noble example of self-sacrifice set by such as Captain H. Gallaugher, D.S.O., who, although severely wounded, continued to fight on, will set us all an example of how a true soldier can meet his death fighting for his King and Country. And adding fresh honour to the laurels already won by his

Battalion. His life and gallant end is an example to us of the true spirit of continuing to fight on until this war is satisfactorily concluded." Writing to Mr. Gallaugher personally the Commanding Officer says, Captain Gallaugher's loss is most keenly felt by us. He was universally beloved and was one of the finest characters I have ever met. He was a true soldier, a great leader and organiser."

Mr. Gallaugher has received the following telegram:

The King and Queen deeply regret the loss you and the Army have sustained by the death of your son in the service of his Country. Their Majesties truly sympathise with you in your sorrow.

Addressing the Grand Jury at the Lifford Crown Sessions His Honour Judge Cooke said that Captain Gallaugher was one of the typical instances of the men who had gone from Co. Donegal to fight and, if he might say so, was one of themselves. He had the pleasure of meeting Captain Gallaugher just before he left for France at the review of the Brigade by the Lord Lieutenant. He deeply sympathised with his Father and family in their bereavement.

Preaching in First Ray Presbyterian Church, Manorcunningham, on Sabbath morning, the Rev. S. Watson, B.A., read the congregation the following letter from Captain Rev. Dr. E. J. McKee, Minister of the Church who was serving as Chaplain with the Ulster Division:-

This letter is dictated to you in loving memory of the late Captain Henry Gallaugher, D.S.O., Royal Inniskilling Fusiliers, who was killed in action on the morning of the 7th June. I write with mingled feelings of deep sorrow and great pride, and I know that First Ray will hear with deep regret and sorrow of his death, but be truly proud of the heroic manner in which he fell on a victorious battlefield. For me he was the link between my work at home and abroad - "liaison" between that as Pastor and that as Captain. When the hour 3.10 a.m. arrived, and he led his Company over the top, ten minutes would have brought me to his side, as my Battalion was close to his. During those early hours of the struggle from darkness to light, from battle to victory - my thoughts were with him, and I know that he would be foremost in the leadership of the day that went so well for the Division of which he was so proud. I was not surprised to hear afterwards that he had been hit in the arm early in the action, but continued to lead his men to their objective, simply remarking "One of my wings is gone". Later, when his work was done, he was hit again and his spirit soared up to the God that called it forth. Words are such feeble instruments to express the sense of loss sustained by his death or to enshrine the glorious spirit of one who was so brave and true and good in life and death. He was the Happy Warrior. One of God's own volunteers, who said from the beginning, "Here am I, send me to every call of duty or need". It was characteristic of Henry Gallaugher that his great desire was to lead his own Company to their objective, and to no other would he give this honour when such an opportunity presented itself. In spite of the consequences we must not regret the decision that embodied such a high and noble spirit, for in that he was, as ever, true to his own self and he could not act otherwise. He carried that bright, cheery smile that was part of his nature, into the hour of battle, and the last words he said to me were, "We don't worry Doctor, do we?" The happy smile on his face had a vital connection with the light of God's love in his heart, and with the simple trust in the God that doeth all things well. It was this fact that made him so ready to go to the land afar off. Now in a Cemetery on the Battlefield which I created the same day he fell, his body lies, but his soul is at peace there, near to the spot where he made the supreme sacrifice I buried him who is so dear to all our hearts, in the evening hour of the day after the battle of the 7th June. On the morn of the battle he had set his face towards the rising sun as was the line of direction. "The night is dark, and I am far from home, Lead thou me on. O'er moor and fen, o'er crag and torrent till the night is gone. And with the morn those angel faces smile which I have loved long since and lost awhile." He had been led into the light of God's presence by the Son of righteousness with healing in his wings. "Thanks be unto God who giveth us the victory through our Lord Jesus Christ." The Union Jack - the flag for which Henry Gallaugher died - was his shroud, and a wooden Cross marks his grave. The Cross of his Master had been laid on his life and borne with heroic courage and Christian cheerfulness, and would to God that we all carried ours in the same noble spirit.

This is a copy of the list of recommendations following the battle.

<u>11th (S.) BATTN. ROYAL INNISKILLING FUSILIERS.</u>
<u>RECOMMENDATIONS FOR IMMEDIATE REWARD IN ORDER OF MERIT</u>

	Recommended for
Captain H. Gallaugher, D.S.O.	V.C.
(Killed in action)	(posthumous)
Captain W.M. Knight	D.S.O.

Captain G.M. Forde   BAR to M.C.
Acting Captain S. Fluke   M.C.
2nd Lieut. W.J.C. Tunstall   M.C.
Captain Rev. A. Spence (Chaplain C. of I. attached)   M.C.

Other Ranks

No. 8893 Sergt. Greaves, J.   D.C.M.
No. 14481 Sergt. Parke, J.   D.C.M.
No. 14058 Corpl. Edwards, J.R.   M.M.
No. 14895 L/Cpl. Muir, W.   M.M.
No. 18315 L/Cpl. Gardner, W.   M.M.
No. 9860 Sergt. Owens, R. J.   M.M.
No. 14091 Sergt. McClintock, R.   M.M.
No. 43069 Pte. Garrity, A.   M.M.
No. 29097 Pte. Meeke, J.   M.M.
No. 28980 Pte. McGee, P.   M.M.
No. 16828 Pte. Beatty, J. R.   M.M.
No. 17245 L/Cpl. McClintock, T.   M.M.

A.C. Pratt, Lieut. Col.
Commanding 11th (S.) Bn. Rl. Inniskilling Fus.

In the Field
14th June, 1917.

THIS IS TO CERTIFY

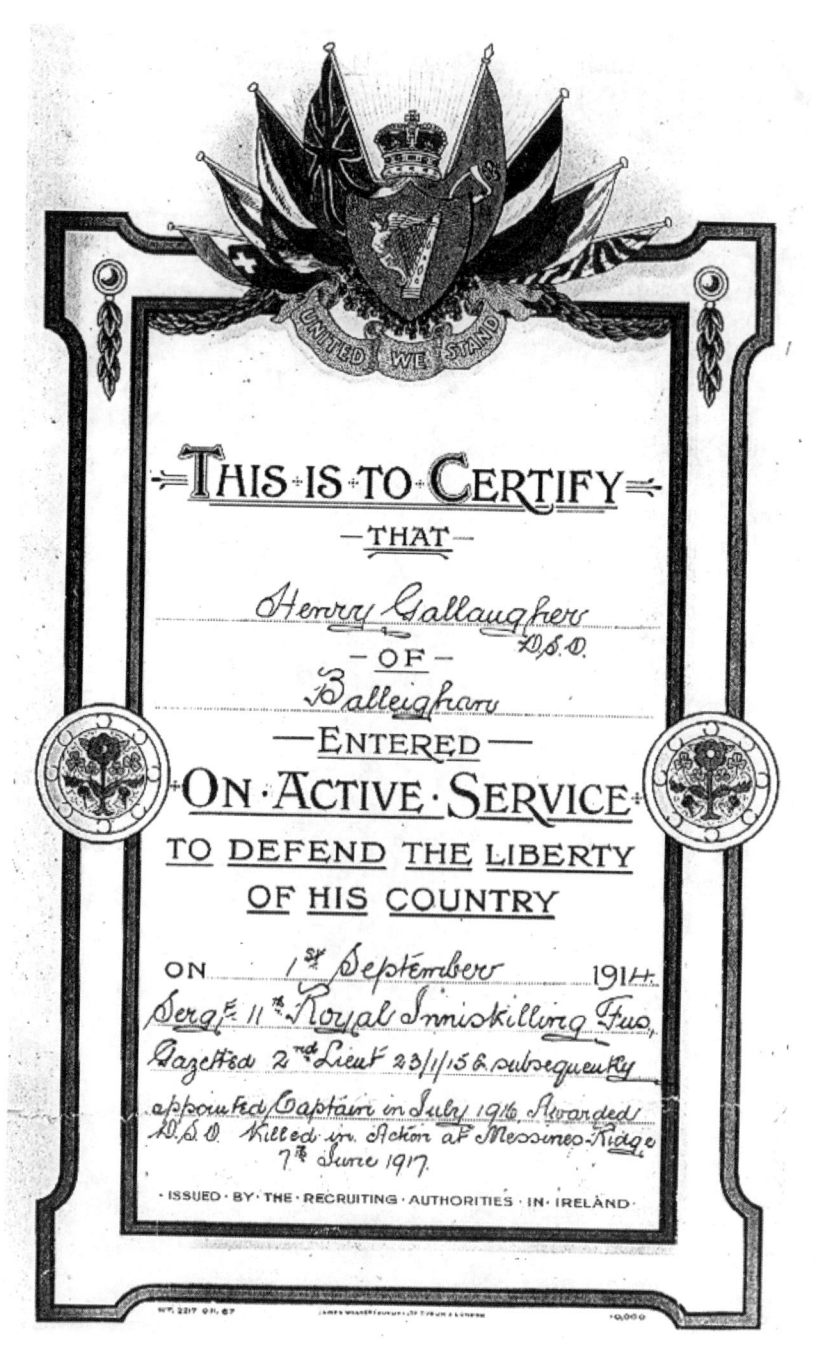

—THAT—

Henry Gallaugher D.S.O.

—OF—

Balleighan

—ENTERED—

ON ACTIVE SERVICE

TO DEFEND THE LIBERTY
OF HIS COUNTRY

ON 1st September 1914.
Sergt. 11th Royal Inniskilling Fus,
Gazetted 2nd Lieut 23/1/15 & subsequently
appointed Captain in July 1916 Awarded
D.S.O. Killed in Action at Messines-Ridge
7th June 1917.

· ISSUED · BY · THE · RECRUITING · AUTHORITIES · IN · IRELAND ·

CHAPTER 21

Passchendaele - Fighting in the Mud

Many a weary season had passed since the loyal lads of Ulster came streaming in from town and countryside fired with enthusiasm for the great cause. Those were happy days full of the promise of action and great achievements. A promise which had been fulfilled in the stirring record of the Eleventh.

In many ways the glamour had faded now but the spirit which bound them together still remained.

The previous losses meant there were now many strange faces in the Battalion and by now many Englishmen had joined its ranks.

One Englishman said that when he first joined he was sure the Irishmen were very jealous of the reputation of their Battalion and would resent them. Finding that they were so well received he concluded "I think we were very lucky to be transferred to a Battalion where the men were so well treated and looked after in every respect".

The Sprig - the Regimental Journal - noted that there was an expectation of the swiftly approaching downfall of the enemy. After nineteen months the fighting spirit of the Eleventh was unimpaired. That spirit which brought them through all their tragic experiences remained no less inspiring and real.

The Eleventh had a number of "characters". One of them was Davis Hamilton who was awarded the M.M. He kept a dog called Hoozle which followed him everywhere. Sadly Hoozle was killed and Davis survived to be given the dog's name which stuck with him all his life.

He returned to Derrygonnelly and had a colourful life as barber, gravedigger and postman to name but a few.

Early in July Capt. S. Myles was wounded and taken off strength.

The Eleventh endured a few more long marches and on the "Twelfth" they were at Alquines. Once again Capt. Crosbie organised a splendid sports day in celebration of the occasion. At one o'clock the field was crowded with all sorts and conditions of men including representatives of other units.

Capt. Crosbie was very aware of the need to give the men an outlet for their energies. In a very practical way he ensured that healthy competition occupied the mind and body. The strain of the recent battle would be relieved by this activity. A race course with every modern athletic device had been prepared. The splendid programme of sports and the results testified to the talent within the Eleventh.

Many locals were present including the Mademoiselle Concheviel and other charming ladies. Apparently they all coped with the soldiers' French with great patience.

The most exciting event of the day was the childrens' one hundred yards handicap. There were many favourites and large sums were wagered.

Little Roger of the Estaminet, paced by the R.S.M., was the winner.

The Rev. Dr. McKee and Dr. McBurey excelled in the three legged race. In a pillow fight over water, Langlet, the original farmer's boy in true Gaullic style defeated all comers.

Altogether there were over twenty different events and the Commanding Officer distributed the prizes.

Previously there had been a lively Brigade football league with R.S.M. Bleakley M.C.being prominent in the organising of the games.

It was learned that L/Cpl. Willie Rutledge from Manorhamilton was awarded the M.M. for his bravery on June 7th. He had compelled forty of the enemy to surrender and afterwards had carried some of his wounded comrades off the battlefield under heavy fire.

At home in County Antrim Miss Margaret Hamilton had applied for a court order presuming the death of her brother 2nd. Lt. John Hamilton in action. A letter from the Chaplain the Rev. J.J. Wright from Ballyshannon told how 2nd. Lt. Hamilton had been struck by a bullet in the left side of his neck and killed. The Judge said that there was no doubt of the death of this young officer and granted the application.

Capt. D.E. Crosbie M.C. was transferred to 110 Field Ambulance on July 23rd. Everyone in the Eleventh was sorry that the doctor who was ever mindful of their welfare was leaving them. His heroic work at the Somme was a byword in the Eleventh.

Happily Capt. Crosbie M.C. survived the war and went on to make a significant contribution to the welfare of the people of Londonderry. He served as Consultant in the Eye and Ear Hospital and amongst other appointments was medical officer for the R.U.C.

The Eleventh reached the final of the Brigade football competition and lost one goal to nil to the 14th R.I.R.

In preparation for the forthcoming battle several large exercises were held. The weather was very wet and on one exercise the Eleventh were inspected by General Sir Hubert Gough. He had replaced General Plumer. Following the Battle of Messines there was no more cheap ground gained from the enemy in the dogged battles for the Heights. The Third Battle of Ypres, probably the most ghastly of the war, was now beginning.

The soldiers had to advance through country which was foul mud against positions of great strength. They were desperately held because they were vital to the enemy.

Most movement at the beginning was on roads and after that along constructed duckboard wooden tracks. To leave these meant almost certain death in the mud. Tanks could not help and the enemy fire swept every road and track.

The enemy had now been forced to realise that the days of successful trench warfare were over. The Battle of Arras had taught him that and he now prepared for defence in depth using shell crater nests, tunnels and pill boxes held by groups of men and machine-guns.

To bring the Eleventh up to strength a draft of seventy two men arrived in the last week of July.

Nearly everyone who had been put up for awards following the battle of Messines received them. At a combined Church service the G.O.C. of the 36th Division presented the following with the ribbon of the M.M.

C.S.M. Greaves J., Sgt. Parke J. and Sgt. Gardiner W., Pte. McGhee P. and Pte. Beatty J.R.

Capt. G.M. Forde received a bar to his M.C. and Capt. W.M. Knight was awarded the M.C.

In showery weather on July 30th the Eleventh marched to Watou and arrived after midnight. They spent an uncomfortable night in tents.

The next day was spent awaiting orders for the offensive. On that showery day the strength of the Eleventh was thirty five officers and eight hundred and eighty men.

During the previous six weeks the Germans had built up their defences again. The delay after Messines was due mainly to the French troops attached to some British formations not being prepared. Several objectives were located well into enemy held ground and the area in between was a quagmire. The shelling had destroyed the ground and the whole drainage system. With bad weather the soldiers were going into a hellish situation.

On the first day of August there was an intense bombardment by our Artillery. The Eleventh were on two hours' notice to move but this was cancelled because of the very wet weather.

Next the Battalion moved to Wieltje area and were under command of 107 Bde. This brigade was holding the front and support lines. The Eleventh occupied the line north side of Saint Jean - Weiltje road. The trenches were in very poor condition owing to the wet weather.

Capt. C.B. Falls was transferred to the staff of the 36th Division on August 15th. Later he served on the staff of the 62nd Division and as liaison officer with the French.

The Eleventh moved back to Vlamertinghe and again were living in tents. They remained there to August 14th when they marched back to Wieltje to take part in the offensive. They took over their old trenches again. These were known as Durham and Admiral trenches. B and C Coys were in the front line.

On the night of August 15th the Eleventh went in to the assembly trenches. A and D Coys took over the Black line from 8 Royal Irish Rifles.

B and C Coys were in support in the old front line trenches Durham, Armitage and Admiral. Carrying parties were in Bilge trench along with Battalion Headquarters.

There was a heavy bombardment and it grew in ferocity on the following day. Six men were wounded and one was killed.

At zero hour on August 16th the Eleventh attacked. The 14 R.I.R. were on the right and the 1-5 Gloucesters on the left.

A Company were on the right, D Coy on the left as the attack went in. There was a four platoon frontage about four hundred yards across. Almost immediately the Commanding Officer Lt. Col. Pratt D.S.O. was wounded by a shell at Battalion Headquarters. He died fifteen minutes later and Major D.E. Knott D.S.O. took command.

The Eleventh were to take the Green line and wait for the second wave to pass through to the dotted Green line. The final objective was the Red line. In support were the 9th and 10th Inniskillings. No Stokes mortars could be carried forward to support the attack because the ground was like a bog.

Nevertheless, the planning for this attack bore the Inniskilling hallmark of presenting detailed orders with simplicity. The Commanding Officer had briefed all the officers thoroughly and platoons and sections had similar briefings.

Defined platoons were to consolidate on specific points of the objective for all round defence. Efforts were to be concentrated on enemy strong points which had not been destroyed by artillery fire. Portions of trenches and patches ground of tactical value for providing cross fire over intervening spaces were to be seized.

A section of tanks was to be used for mopping up if they could be employed at all because of the terrible mud.

A white signallers flag with the Castle of Inniskilling in blue with XI below it was to be carried. Only to be used to identify the Eleventh position in extreme cases. Battalion Headquarters was located in Wieltje mine shaft.

The final objective was the portion of the Gheluvelt - Langemarck line between the forward boundaries and included Aviatik Farm.

The Officer Commanding A Coy ordered two sections to help the 14th R.I.R. capture Schuler Farm. The battle of Langemarck had begun.

Heavy shelling was experienced for an hour and a half and all the Battalion Headquarters signallers' equipment was destroyed. Lt. McComb, the Signals Officer, had an unenviable task.

Zero hour was 4.45 a.m. and began with an intense bombardment. The advance began as the barrage lifted but the state of the ground made it very difficult. Men were up to their knees in the mud.

The machine-gun fire of the enemy was intense and accurate. Pill boxes were intact and had to be dealt with in detail.

A Coy came under heavy machine-gun fire from Caserne. The enemy machine-guns were not neutralised by the bombardment. There were many casualties with men struggling in the terrible mud to help fallen comrades. The Eleventh were channelled into a killing ground.

A small group of eight men and an officer reached the green line but were finally pinned down by heavy machine-gun fire. A messenger sent back to give their position was killed. This very brave party was so isolated and without support they were forced to wait and withdraw that night. They could do no more.

Capt. Irvine's company was advancing steadily in the face of effective enemy fire. In particularly nasty circumstances they had been forced to shelter in shell holes. L/Cpl. Willie Rutledge M.M. from Manorhamilton had been helping to dress the wounds of several men showing an absolute disregard of danger.

From the shell holes the Company Commander saw some of his men advancing too far on the right. Willie Rutledge ran forward and said that he would warn them. He dashed forward through a hail of machine-gun fire and fell mortally wounded. Capt. Irvine tried to help him but seeing it was impossible to save his life gave him morphine to ease his pain.

D Company had met fierce opposition from the Caserne and were pinned down for some time. They finally stormed this particular position, Fort Hill, and destroyed it.

C was the left support company and became split up. Some were embroiled in the attack on Caserne and the remainder with the Company Commander were further forward but were held up by enfilade fire from Pond Farm. About twenty men were left when the Company Commander was killed - a few of the survivors crawled back.

The right support company suffered heavily as well. They had come under fire from four positions including Pond Farm and Caserne. Finally connection was made on the left and they consolidated Fort Hill.

The after battle report states that even had little opposition been met because of the terrible mud it prevented the platoons keeping up with the barrage. The pill boxes and enemy wire were still intact and a battle had to be fought for every strong point.

The enemy shelled the valley of the Steenbeck very heavily throughout the day and the following night.

The Eleventh had made a costly sacrifice. Four officers and forty soldiers were killed. Six officers and one hundred and seventy one men were wounded. One officer and forty one men were missing.

The whole brigade had paid very dearly. The dead lay in trenches and in No Man's Land. The stench was horrible as many could not be recovered for burial because of the mud and water.

In the wider context General Nugent felt great sorrow at what he then believed to be the failure of the Ulster Division. He was later reassured when he learned the other divisions in the attack were stopped as well.

The Battle of Langemarck was the second of the series of engagements in the Third Battle of Ypres, which, beginning on July 31st, did not end till December. It brought some improvements in position at dreadful cost and diverted the Germans' attention from the southern part of the Allies line.

Weary after this exhausting battle the Eleventh moved to tents at Vlamertinghe only to be ordered to Winnizeele that evening August 17th. They travelled by motor lorries thankful there was a break from the interminable marching.

Resting here for the next five days also involved much routine work and the sad task of inspecting the kits of the casualties.

On August 23rd the Battalion went by train to Bapaume and marched to camp a mile north of Barastre.

Here there was refitting and bathing until they relieved the Royal Scots.

R.Q.M.S. Brock was rewarded for all his dedicated work by being granted a Quartermaster's Commission and the rank of Lieutenant.

At the same time news was received that Pte. W. Owens had received the prestigious award of the Meritorious Service Medal.

In the confusion of war it was often very difficult to contact relatives for various reasons. One such case was Pte. James Graham. He was taken to a Casualty Clearing Station in the early morning and died of his wounds on October 22nd. The only identification on him was a letter from some of his friends in Lettercran L.O.L. 1269. The Matron wrote to the Lodge and asked the members to pass on the tragic news to his relatives.

In the previous week over fifty men had arrived in drafts and the strength of the Eleventh stood at twenty seven officers and six hundred and forty two other ranks.

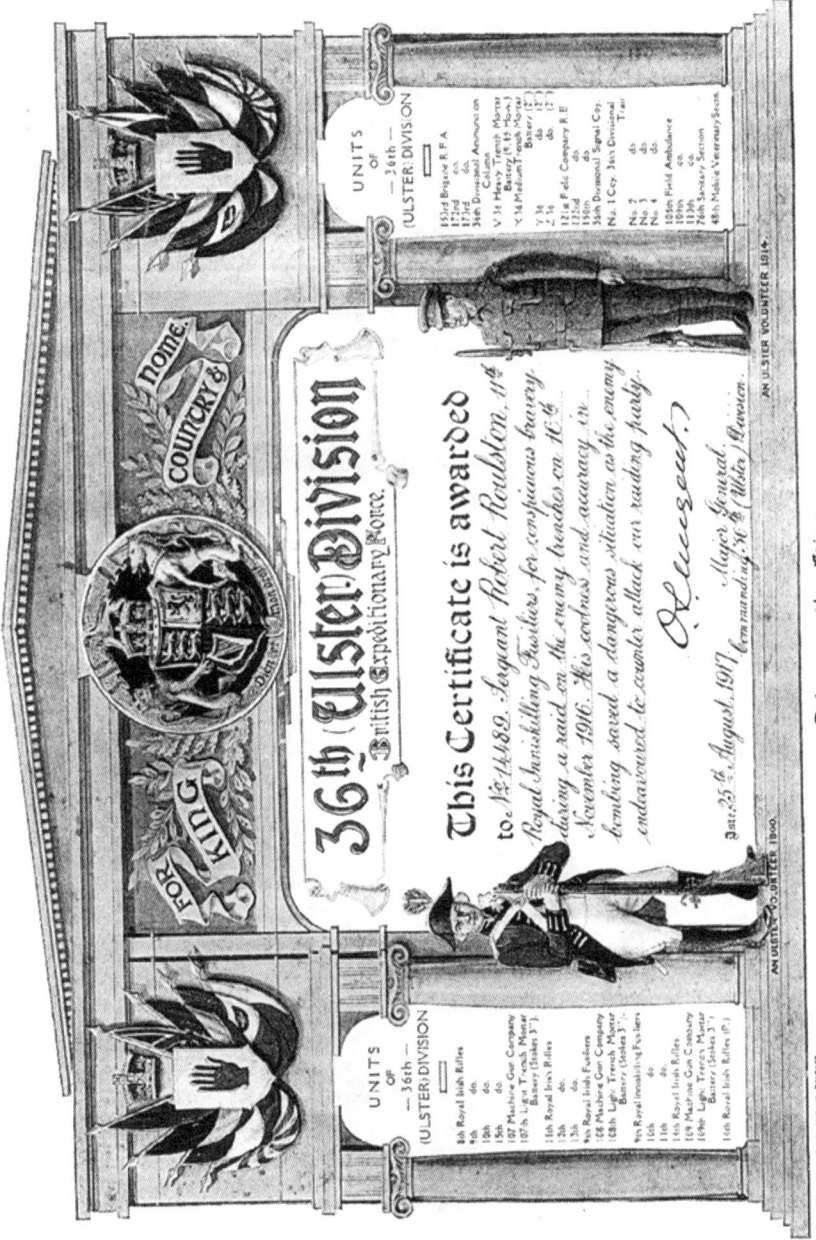

36th (Ulster) Division
British Expeditionary Force.

This Certificate is awarded to No. 14482 Sergeant Robert Roulston, 11th Royal Inniskilling Fusiliers, for conspicuous bravery during a raid on the enemy trenches on 16th November 1916. His coolness and accuracy in bombing saved a dangerous situation as the enemy endeavoured to counter attack on raiding party.

O. Nugent (?)
Major General
Commanding 36th (Ulster) Division

Date 25th August 1917.

UNITS OF — 36th — (ULSTER) DIVISION

153rd Brigade R.F.A.
122nd do.
173rd do.
36th Divisional Ammunition Column
Y.36 Heavy Trench Mortar Battery (R.H.S. How.)
V.36 Medium Trench Mortar Battery (P)
Y.36 do. (P)
Z.36 do. (P)
121st Field Company R.E.
122nd do.
150th do.
36th Divisional Signal Coy.
No. 1 Coy. 36th Divisional Train
No. 2 do.
No. 3 do.
No. 4 do.
108th Field Ambulance
109th do.
110th do.
76th Sanitary Section
48th Mobile Veterinary Section

8th Royal Irish Rifles
9th do.
10th do.
15th do.
107 Machine Gun Company
107a Light Trench Mortar Battery (Stokes 3")
11th Royal Irish Rifles
12th do.
13th do.
9th Royal Irish Fusiliers
108 Machine Gun Company
108 Light Trench Mortar Battery (Stokes 3")
9th Royal Inniskilling Fusiliers
14th Royal Irish Rifles
109 Machine Gun Company
109b Light Trench Mortar Battery (Stokes 3")
16th Royal Irish Rifles (P.)

God save the King.

CHAPTER 22

Refitting and Training

Following a week in the trenches at the beginning of September the Eleventh went in to Brigade reserve.

The next week at Bertincourt there was a mixed menu of training, fitting out and bathing. The usual working parties had to be found.

Some of the men found it almost a waste of time to participate in training after all they had been through. However, as in every group of young men there were those jokers who made light of the situation.

It was officially announced that the M.M. had been awarded to Sgt. Warren Cpls. Stett J., Elliott W. and Johnston S. Ptes. Donnell S., Orgill F. and Ferguson W. Orgill had previously been awarded the Ulster Division Certificate.

The M.C. was awarded to Capt. G.M.F. Irvine 2nd. Lt. Sweeny T.C. and the Rev. A. Spence. All these were for their good work in recent operations.

Thomas Sweeny's citation reads:

"For conspicuous gallantry and devotion to duty. When the advance was held up, during an attack, he led a bombing section against an enemy machine-gun, which he captured, killing two of the crew and wounding the remainder. Although badly wounded, he continued to direct the operations of his platoon until the position was entirely gained. His coolness and example were a great inspiration to the men."

About this time Lt. A. S. Robinson U.S. Medical Corps. was attached to the Eleventh. This was an unusual situation but it is believed it was because he had close family ties with the Eleventh.

The Eleventh remained in the Hermies sector until the end of October. They were mainly in Brigade reserve relieving the 9th Inniskillings on three occasions during which only one man was wounded.

Major Whitlas and several other officers joined the Battalion for duty. In this number were 2nd. Lts. W. Baker, G. Milne, J.M. Robinson, H. Buckley, H. Legg,

A. Hughes, J. Gray and R. Abraham.

By this time Lord Letrim had become Secretary to The Minister for the Colonies.

A keen and humourous interest was displayed in the detail that the Q.M. had officers pyjamas available for ten shillings a suit.

The Regimental history recorded that the spirit of the soldier was such that when relieved from the line for a day or two his first idea was to organise a football match.

In the evening, the man who the night before was lurking in a listening post in the mud with a bomb in his hand, was happy if the chance came to mind the baby or help to cook the dinner in a family's home. With courage and endurance he had the sense of humour to meet all things cheerfully.

They were dear souls these soldiers. Brave in battle but not plaster saints. Men with human frailties but with sober strength of soul and kindness of heart.

CHAPTER 23

Cambrai

The Eleventh were in the trenches on the first day of November.

In the second week of November the weather was fine and dry. The Eleventh were engaged in construction work.

Havrincourt Wood was crammed with camouflaged huts. They were building roads by day and by night. During this road building at night Joe Wallace and his friends found it very hard to light their pipes. A break for a pipe had to be taken in a well concealed place. The whole area was rolling country and thick woods. It was a pleasant place but there were no civilians. Heavy ground mists masked observation from the air.

Several new officers had joined the Battalion when it went back to Velu Wood. Here the Battalion was once again accommodated in tents and bivouacs.

Extensive refitting and training occupied them for the three days before the offensive. Once again the outward cheerfulness and camaraderie belied the personal tensions before the attack.

It is useful to consider the background to this attack in which the Eleventh played a vital part.

Following the Somme the enemy had withdrawn several miles in the spring of 1917 to the Hindenburg Line. It had been built by thousands of Russian prisoners used as forced labour. Having many deep underground bunkers and machine-gun positions with superb fields of fire, plus barbed wire in great depth the enemy believed it was impregnable.

The depth of the wire, seventy yards in some places, meant it would not be destroyed by artillery fire. This would have a devastating effect on the Infantry being held up in the advance and destroyed by enemy machine-gun fire in selected killing ground.

The plan was to use tanks to sweep away the concentrations of barbed wire making gaps for the Infantry to push through. Some of the troops saw the tanks for the first time in their lives concealed in the countryside all around.

In this area was the Canal du Nord which the French were building prior to the war. There were huge mounds of earth or spoil heaps from the bed of the canal. Strong points had been constructed by the enemy out of the great mounds of earth. For possession of two of these spoil heaps there were frequent raids and counter raids during the stages of preparation for the Battle of Cambrai.

In essence the 36th Division had a one Brigade task and this was allocated to the Inniskilling Brigade the 109th. The German trenches were to be captured west of the Canal du Nord and south of the Bapaume Road in front of Graincourt. As soon as the canal crossing was secured a bridge was to be built - strong enough to carry all artillery and wagons - on the Demicourt to Flesquieres road. A lighter bridge would be constructed further south.

The Brigade plan was to seize the spoil heap on its northern front. From this machine-guns and trench mortars would dominate the enemy and cover the assault of the troops clearing the German trench lines. To ensure the rate of advance would not be slowed down Lewis gun teams were used in co-operation with the bombers at the head of each platoon. The great width of the Hindenburg trenches ensured there were no bottlenecks.

At one o'clock in the morning the Eleventh left Velu Wood and occupied their assembly trenches. There was no interruption and equipment was issued to the troops. This included extra ammunition for Lewis guns, bombs, hedging gloves and wire cutters. Bomb throwers had fifty rounds of ammunition and six bombs. The rifle bomb squad carriers also had a bucket with twelve bombs. The rifle grenadiers had fifty rounds of ammunition and an additional ten rifle grenades each. Altogether this made a formidable arsenal.

Having rested until ordered to move to the attack the Eleventh followed swiftly on the heels of the Tyrones.

A few casualties were sustained on the move up. Capt. Knight was commanding A Coy plus a platoon of B Coy and he led his men quickly up the 'C' trench northwards along the Canal du Nord. When dugouts and trenches had been cleared to save duplication of effort a notice board was positioned with the one word "Mopped"

The plan was developing well. By not using open ground, but fighting through, clearing and advancing along enemy trenches, protection from fire was assured.

Beginning two hours after the main attack and with no designated artillery bombardment beforehand the aim was speed and surprise.

At 8.30 a.m. the artillery bombardment began with great ferocity and continued to plaster registered targets in the fire plan. The trench mortars fired thermite incendiary shells for four minutes.

Leading D Coy was 2nd. Lt. R. S. Barrowman. They quickly moved up the German support line.

Capt. W. H. Wagentreiber from Lifford - known affectionately to all his men as Willy Wag - commanded C Coy. They worked swiftly up the German front line.

Capt. Wagentreiber who had been wounded in July 1916 survived the war and became a prominent figure in County Donegal. He was connected with several public bodies and was for many years a member of Donegal County Council. He had been a Company Commander in the Ulster Volunteers.

Ahead the 9th Inniskillings were meeting stiff resistance from machine-guns in the A and C trenches of the enemy. Capt. Wagentreiber and C Coy became involved and sharp fighting ensued. Four men of C Coy had killed eight of their opponents who were resisting fiercely with bombs and machine-guns. Here the work of the rifle grenadiers was of great value.

A and D Coy dashed forward and passed through the Tyrones position. All morning the weather was foul. At ten past one in the afternoon A and D Coy had arrived at Lock No. 6 where they were held up by machine-gun fire.

On the east side of the canal there were troops of the 62nd Division being held up from the same place and were behind men of the Eleventh.

2nd Lt. J. Finney went back and arranged with them to send forward two tanks. This was quickly achieved and the enemy fled over the Spoil Heap hotly fired on by A Coy. Lewis gun which inflicted a number of casualties. Shouldering their equipment and with weapons at the ready both companies pushed forward to their objective.

About half past three that afternoon C Coy leap frogged the 9th Inniskillings at their objective. Encountering little resistance they reached their position as darkness was falling an hour later.

An immediate reorganisation took place to consolidate the position and provide defence in depth. C and D Coy held the objective. A Coy were on a line one hundred and fifty yards south of the Bapaume - Cambrai road with Battalion

Headquarters nearby.

Determined to make their presence felt the Eleventh sent out strong patrols that night. They went northwards up the trenches towards Moeuvres. In bold Inniskilling tradition going forward to meet danger rather than await it. Only one patrol met any resistance and was driven back by rifle fire. No further opposition was encountered and no counter attack took place that night.

In the early morning of November 21st the remainder of the brigade passed through the Eleventh's position and advanced on Moeuvres. However, their attack was not successful because of heavy machine-gun fire from the village and enemy trenches to the west.

An advance of the line by a thousand yards was the net result of the day's work. Casualties of the Eleventh were six soldiers killed, an officer and twenty five soldiers wounded.

That night the Inniskilling Battalions were withdrawn from the line and the Eleventh remained in Hermies for the few days' rest.

After two more days in the trenches the Battalion marched to billets in Bertincourt and Doignies.

It was hoped the men would get a few weeks rest at this juncture but that was not to be.

J. W. Charlton enlisted on 7th Sept 1914 at Enniskillen and went to Finner Camp to join the Eleventh on the 22nd Sept. He was immediately appointed Acting Sergeant in 'A' Coy and was made Substantive Sergeant a month later.

On 19th April 1915 he was commissioned and following several courses was appointed Assistant Adjutant of the 12th Battalion.

He was married at Carlow on 22nd Dec 1915. In September 1916 he was posted to the 9th Battalion in France.

Having been wounded at Messines, hospitalised and awarded the M.C. he returned to the Eleventh at the front in November 1917.

Returning to the 9th Battalion at the end of 1917 he was promoted to Captain and earned a bar to the M.C. in May and the Croix de Guerre in December 1918.

He later wrote a detailed summary of his service in an old cash book.

The last day of November saw the Eleventh on another long gruelling route march in torrential ruin. The high morale of the Battalion kept everyone in shape during this slog of over seven hours. Arriving at Achiet-la-Petit at half past ten that night, they rested in tents, wet and weary.

CHAPTER 24

The Unkept Promise

Having endured the terrible weather in the latter end of November the whole division had moved back to the promise of some weeks rest out of the line. This promise could not be kept because the great enemy counter offensive had broken in to the southern part of the line.

For the first few days of December the Eleventh were on the move again.

On December 3rd the Battalion was at Bertincourt standing by to move at a moment's notice. The next day they moved at nine o'clock to Havrincourt Wood. Having had their dinner they moved off again in the afternoon to the Hindenburg support line.

The next move was to relieve the 9th Inniskillings at Welsh Ridge. They had suffered very heavily in the German counter attack and lost all their company commanders. The Tyrones, as they were known, were but a remnant now.

In this position the Donegals were very heavily shelled. A daring counter attack was successfully carried out at 6 a.m. The Eleventh cleared three hundred yards of trench on a two hundred yard front. Contact was made with the Battalions right and left. This vigorous action straightened out an important sector of the line. The enemy was driven off the crest of Welsh Ridge. All the ground gained was successfully held despite two heavy counter attacks inside four hours. Seven soldiers were killed and eleven wounded. Welsh Ridge was safe for the time being.

The next day the position was bombarded by artillery and trench mortars. One man was killed and seven were wounded. After this the Eleventh were relieved by the 10th R.I.R. and went back to the original front line.

The next few days were spent at Mertz. There were more working parties to be provided and those not directly involved got some rest.

Then there was an alarm that the enemy intended to attack in strength in the early hours of the morning. The whole Battalion was ready to move at six o'clock. This did not happen and the Eleventh moved back to Sorel-le-Grand in the afternoon. The march back took place in a snow blizzard, the most severe that had been seen in the area for many years.

The next few days enabled the men to get some rest and helped them to get cleaned up. After a couple more moves the Eleventh were in camp at Lucheux on December 17th. They remained here resting and getting some recreation for the next couple of weeks. This time was taken up by routine work in camp, medical inspections and recreational training.

On December 24th time was actually available to prepare for the festivities of Christmas Day.

A very well attended Church service in the morning put the stamp on an enjoyable Christmas Day. The whole of the Eleventh then assembled for Christmas Dinner and a jolly occasion it turned out to be with the officers serving the men. Once again much of the fare on the tables supplied by the Comforts Fund so ably organised by Mrs. Hessey. This was followed by entertainment provided by the Divisional Follies which caused much mirth and merriment in the audience.

The Commanding Officer spoke to all the men. He thanked them for their willing support and loyalty during the recent operations. He wished every Officer, N.C.O. and man a Happy Christmas and the best of good luck for 1918.

Once again, on December 27th, the Eleventh received notification of awards to its men for their courage and devotion to duty. Sgt. J.R. Edwards was given a Bar to the M.M.

The Military Medal was awarded to Sgt. G. Dick and Sgt. R. Armstrong. The following Privates received the Military Medal, R. Neill, A. C. Godfrey, O. Tulip, H. Law, T. Keyes and J. Tiesseman. Cpl. Fawkes L/Cpl. W. Eames and L/Cpl. Gregory also received the Military Medal.

Lt. J. W. Charlton M.C. was transferred to the 9th Inniskillings and Lt. D. J. Bell joined for duty as Quartermaster.

At the end of the month the Eleventh still had an impressive strength of fifty nine officers and six hundred and seventy one men.

The following letters of congratulation reflect again the gallantry and high esteem in which the Battalion was held within the Division.

Confidential
109th Inf. Bde.
No. S.C. 12/8OL
11th Royal Innis. Fus.

The Divisional Commander directed me to forward the attached letter, and to request that it be treated as confidential.

I beg to congratulate the Battalion on receiving such a satisfactory letter, and not the least gratifying is the commendation of the record of the Regiment of ROYAL INNISKILLING FUSILIERS.

The Regimental Motto of "Nec Aspera Terrent" has been acted up to.

W.G. Hessey
Brig. General
Commanding 109th Inf. Brigade
36th (Ulster) Division
27th December 1917

Confidential
To O.C. 11th R. Inniskilling Fusiliers

I wish to express through you to the Officers and men of the 11th R. Inniskilling Fusiliers how much I value their gallant service form the 20th November until their withdrawal into reserve on the 8th December.
Both in attack and defence the Battalion has consistently maintained its high record of service and devotion.

Under condition of extreme hardship, of cold and fatigue, the Battalion has maintained a high spirit and has cheerfully endured all the discomforts inseparable from the conditions under which the offensive was carried out.

The Battalion has responded to all demands in a manner worthy of the best traditions of the Army and has sustained the high standard of performance reached by the Inniskilling Fusiliers in every position its Battalions have undertaken since the beginning of the war.

26.12.17
O.S.W. NUGENT, Maj. Gen.
Commanding 36th (Ulster) Division.

CHAPTER 25

The System Still Works

With its alternation of victory and reverse the Battle of Cambrai was one of the great dramas of military history. It began with great triumph for the British Army, it continued with frustration and disappointment that brilliant success should be robbed of its fruits by lack of power to exploit. It ended with a desperate effort to save victory from becoming disaster.

At this time the Eleventh were in reserve and all work and training was undertaken accordingly.

Activity in the first week of January reflected this position. The great problem occupying the minds of those in authority was the dearth of new drafts. The Eleventh were still well up to strength and in the normal run of things would remain in action. January 11th saw the Battalion back in the line.

The usual moves to various locations continued first to Soleate and then St. Simon. Here they relieved the 28th Regt. of the French at Essingy Station and were in Brigade reserve. This was not a straightforward relief because of the language differences. The relief was slow as all details had to be translated from French to English and vice-versa. The French officers took a great deal of time explaining all the points and features of their own and the enemy's positions.

Very quickly the Eleventh set about improving their surroundings.

The Military Medal was awarded to Sgt. T. Cairns, Sgt. A. Nesbitt and Ptes. J. Sweeny and J. Hughes.

Sadly Sgt. Cairns was killed later at the Battle of St. Quentin. He came from Drumsillagh, Letterbreen. He had been a member of the Ulster Volunteer Force and of L.O.L. 347. He had been awarded the Divisional Certificate in 1915 for gallant conduct.

The Eleventh relieved the 9th Inniskillings in the Jeanne d'Arc sub sector on January 17th when two men were wounded. Following their relief on January 21st they went into Brigade support thus relieving the 10th Inniskillings.

During the third week of November many working parties had to be supplied to assist with all the preparations for the next offensive. There was not much rest for these men when in reserve and the working days were long.

An Inniskilling officer at Cambrai noted that in a particular way it was comforting to know that in the midst of all the stress the Army system maintained its close control of every detail. A harassed commander making defensive plans to meet an imminent threat, received an urgent message to submit the names of two men for an agricultural course! Truly the Adjutant never ceased from troubling and the weary were never at rest.

Similarly an officer of the Eleventh writing to the Impartial Reporter said that he enjoyed censoring letters as he always found out something about himself. One of his soldiers writing had put it like this "we have got a new officer and I will tell you more about him next time when I get a green envelope". Green envelopes were not censored.

On an appropriate date, January 27th, the Donegals relieved the Tyrones for the last time in Jeanne d'Arc sub sector. On January 29th they marched to Artemps. Here there was ample opportunity to have hot baths and clean up at the end of January.

CHAPTER 26
Farewell to the Eleventh

The Eleventh had started the month with a total strength of fifty five officers and six hundred and thirty five other ranks.

Those with experience would naturally think that was enough to preserve their identity as a Battalion. Other Battalions had gone into battle with similar numbers.

On the very first day of February 1918 notification was received from the commander of the 36th Division that the Battalion was to be disbanded.

The disappointment and sorrow at this decision was felt very keenly by every officer and man. They had been through hell together. In the shared experience of human endurance and suffering theirs was a truly magnificent record - but now they would soon be no more.

The lack of reinforcements from home combined with the terrible toll of casualties had reduced the strength of the Army.

The convention of the numbering of the Battalions in the order of battle militated significantly against the Eleventh.

A new system of the three Battalion brigade was introduced. In its introduction the convention was that the senior Battalion on the roll would remain thus retaining the original identity of 109th Brigade. This was the 9th Inniskillings. The 1st and 2nd Battalion of the Inniskillings were brought into the Brigade. So 109th Brigade was a completely Inniskilling Brigade.

On January 8th at Villnselve twenty officers and four hundred men transferred to the 9th Inniskillings who were but a remnant of their former selves.

At least this large number would remain with their comrades the Tyrones and be warmly received by them. In other units at amalgamation there was misunderstanding and lack of feeling for those involved. The remainder of the Eleventh remained at routine working parties as a composite company. They worked at Artemps and Grand Seracourt and moved to Cugny on February 20th.

On February 21st - with the exception of the Commanding Officer and the Second in Command - thirty officers and two hundred and nineteen other ranks were amalgamated with the 14th R.I.R. This unit then became 23rd Entrenching Battalion.

Nine Warrant Officers and Staff Sergeants were transferred to base but there is no record of their names. However, R.S.M. Guy Bleakley M.C. eventually joined the 9th Bn. in June 1918. He also survived the War and served in the Corps. of Commissionaires. He had completed twenty four years in the Army. He died in Birmingham aged sixty seven in the Autumn of 1935.

This was the end of the Donegals and it was a sad time for them. All they had been was wiped away as the Army reacted and adjusted to the demands being made on it.

The men thought of the early days at Finner and their march through Fermanagh. The days they had spent at Randalstown and the friendships they had made as inexperienced young men of the farmyards and villages when they had been unmarked by the ravages of war. The loss of so many young men and talented lives would deprive their country and local communities of the skills so essential for the future.

Of course this would not entirely end their service together. Some of them would distinguish themselves in the 9th Inniskillings whence they were transferred.

Commanded by an Inniskilling officer, General Hessey, the 109th Brigade of Inniskilling Battalions would bear the brunt of the attack at St. Quentin. From General to private it would singularly display the highest degree of skill, courage and steadfastness.

In September 1918 Pte. Joseph Noble was awarded the Military Medal. "He took command of the section. When a hostile machine-gun held up the advance he rushed forward at the head of his section and compelled the enemy to retire" the citation reads.

Capt. Curley - whom the writer recalls as forthright in his opinions - also distinguished himself. He saw a German mounted patrol get into the lines at night and promptly riding after them he shot one and dispersed the others. He received the M.C.

Another former officer of the Eleventh who had gained an M.C. in 1917 as a

Captain was Lt. Col. Forde. He went on to command the 9th Inniskillings and was awarded the D.S.O.

His citation dated 15th October 1918 reads as follows.

"For conspicuous gallantry and devotion to duty. In company with another officer he crawled out about 400 yards from the front line under full observation from the enemy lines, and remained out above seven hours, making most daring reconnaissance of the enemy's position, and gaining most valuable information, from which he organised a successful raid on the enemy's position. By his personal courage and coolness he set a splendid example to his Battalion."

This day February 21st 1918 saw the end of the active service life of the Eleventh.

A man's life, a community's life or a Battalion's life is truly measured by the way which it has fulfilled the purpose for which it exists. In this the Eleventh nobly succeeded.

CHAPTER 27

". . . And when the War is over. . ."

As thousands of men were being demobilised those of the Eleventh who had survived after they were transferred were coming home.

What would they find to do in the changing world after the war to end wars? How would they cope and what work would they find to do?

An Ex Serviceman's organisation had been formed to help find work but it met with varying degrees of success depending on the area those returning came from.

Many wanted to seek their fortune farther afield and others still had a spirit of adventure. Scores of these men emigrated and amongst them was Cpl. Joe Wallace. He had tried to settle to farming and other work including the R.U.C. However, the prospects for advancement were not good and he emigrated to New Zealand.

He farmed there until his death on September 23rd 1970. He prospered and had a large family. During the second War he was called up because his record showed he had been a machine-gun instructor.

He served in the New Zealand Army for some time as an Instructor. Eventually his wounds from the Somme, Ypres and St. Quentin began to tell on him and he was discharged in 1943.

L/Cpl. Alex (Clamper) McMullen a native of Ballyshannon had won the M.M. in 1916. He had spent his early working life in the timber trade in Ballyshannon. He retired from the Army in 1938 and became an Inspector with the Special Constabulary in Omagh. At the outbreak of the second War he joined the Home Guard and became Adjutant. He then became Adjutant of the U.S.C. in Co. Derry and was awarded the M.B.E. Years later he often recalled his unbelief and amazement at finding electric light installed by the Germans in their deep fortifications of the Hindenburg line.

L/Cpl. Louis Hazlett D.C.M. M.M. also returned to his Roslea home after the war. He had subsequently gained the M.M. when serving with the Royal Engineers. He continued in the family tradition in the saw mill.

He was married in 1924 to Elizabeth Hazlett - no relation - and set up home in Lisbellaw. They were blessed with four sons and five daughters. Louis was a keen fisherman often wetting the line on a favourite stretch of the Colebrooke River near his home.

Travellers on the narrow road between Killykeeran Cross and Boyhill would often see the grand old soldier on his daily stroll and he had many a cheery word for them.

Capt. James W. Charlton M.C. and bar had been a former pupil of Enniskillen Model School and Portora Royal School. He was demobilised in March 1919.

On returning from the war he attended Queen's University and became B.Sc. Engineering. He was appointed assistant surveyor in Fermanagh. He became Deputy County Surveyor in 1940. He had wide interests among them being Secretary to the Select Vestry of St. McCartin's Cathedral. He was an artist of considerable talent and did much for the development of art in the area. He also served in the Home Guard in the second war and had a keen interest in Scouting. He received the O.B.E. in 1940. His uniform has been preserved by his family and his binoculars clearly show shrapnel scars. The binoculars saved his life by deflecting the shrapnel. He died on 16th January 1957.

Robert Roulston came home to work on the family farm near Newtowncunningham in Co. Donegal. Farming life had changed very little since he had left four years previously.

The young Robert settled down very quickly to the routine of ploughing, milking and making hay - putting behind him the terrible experiences he had come through. However, on the first of July each year he always looked at his watch reflecting for a while on the conditions at that particular time on the Somme in 1916. Life got harder in the twenties and thirties as Ireland struggled with a changing political and economic situation.

The price of cattle was very poor and people struggled to make a living. In fact everything was a bad price and a good bullock would only make £4. His son Robert and his wife and family continue the farming tradition and way of life on the same farm today.

Capt. Cyril Falls, a former pupil of Portora, had been employed at the end of the war to write the History of the 36th Ulster Division. This brought him into contact with those who were writing the official history of the war. He then joined this group in 1923. He remained with it until 1939. Included in his work were the histories of the campaigns in Egypt and Palestine as well as that of Macedonia.

He was a prolific writer. He became military correspondent of The Times in 1939. He had a distinguished career with the paper to 1953. He was elected to the Chicele chair of the history of war at Oxford. He held this post from 1946 to 1953 and he continued to produce a great volume of work in these years.

Falls was a very humane man with a sharp sense of humour, small in stature, always immaculately turned out and with an elegant moustache. He was married to Elizabeth Heath and they had two daughters. He was appointed C.B.E. in 1967. He died on 23rd April 1971. He was a loyal Ulsterman and a gifted member of the Eleventh Inniskillings.

Major Sproule Myles M.C. returned to his home Inis-Samer in Ballyshannon. A man of rare discernment he devoted most of his life to public affairs. His family business was well established. In fact he was the grandson of Robert Myles, an old Inniskilling who had fought at Waterloo.

He became active in local politics and was kidnapped by the Republicans in 1922 and released after a short time.

He was first elected to Dail Eireann in 1923 representing Donegal. He topped the polls in several subsequent elections and served in the Dail to 1943. He was an effective representative and well liked by all sections of the community.

He was active in Donegal County Council for many years. His genial manner meant that his friends could be numbered in hundreds. He was popular and a generous and jovial host. He was one of the first people in Ballyshannon to own a car and it was a little white sports model.

In Masonic circles he was well known and took a great interest in the Order's affairs. He had a great practical interest in his old school Foyle College and made many gifts of books to the library there.

Being a far sighted man he introduced electricity to Ballyshannon in late 1918. This was the first country town to gain this distinction apart from Lisburn even to the extent of street lighting. He died on 13th February 1956 aged 78.

Davy Donaldson also survived and returned to form a thriving business in Derrygonnelly. He had been wounded on his birthday July 1st at the Somme. He had a famous greyhound called Thiepval Glory. It was successful in many races. His residence was called Thiepval House. All his life he bore the scars and wounds of the trenches but this did not deter him starting a new career in very difficult times.

Matt Tiernan farmed all his life on an island in Lough Erne. He was also a successful commercial eel fisherman. He would always bring his bicycle when coming to do business on the shores of Lough Erne. Years later ,when buying cattle, there was often a frequent exchange of remarks in a good natured attempt to influence the price. This was among former comrades, including A. McIlfatrick, referring to incidents in cafes in those now long past off duty periods. No matter how vivid the imagination it did not change the price of the beast.

No. 14733 Pte. John Stephenson returned to the family farm at Ardagh, Co. Donegal. He married Emma Laird Colhoun 20th August 1919 at Carnone, Co. Donegal. The match was not approved of by the bride's family and they eloped after the marriage to Canada. The band on the boat were playing "I'm forever blowing bubbles" on the voyage over. Eventually they returned to farm at Carrigans. He recalled in later years along with Alex Roulston how they were placed at the end of the trenches to prevent men from running away. In the Eleventh this never happened. After the war he used to visit with a fellow Inniskilling James Duffy V.C. They remained friends all their lives.

An ambitious programme for returning soldiers was developed on Cleenish Island on Upper Lough Erne. Farms of above forty acres were given to a dozen returning soldiers. A suitable house was built on each farm.

However the scheme to re-settle the valiant men who served their country eventually failed except in one case. It was a harsh way of life in the early 1920s. To get to the island was by way of a cable operated ferry. A typical Lough Erne cot - which is a flat bottomed boat used to carry cattle or a horse and cart - was propelled by a hand operated windlass along the cable. This was the means of getting from the mainland to the island.

One major mistake was the failure to build a bridge at the time. This and several other factors were reasons for the failure of the island settlement.

In 1925 all the cattle took the fluke. The men had farms but no money coming in. There was a severe rent of £1 an acre and they had all borrowed money from the bank. There were other problems associated with living on an island and the lack of facilities eventually meant that nearly all gave up the farms.

After the second World War several schemes were mooted to build a bridge and at last one was completed. The bridge carries telephone lines, electricity cables and water mains. This was all too late to help the original occupiers.

As was the custom following the War all those Battalions raised for its duration were presented with a King's Colour. Like many others, only the survivors, who were now civilians again would parade to receive them.

The following extract from The Sprig, the Regimental journal which so excellently recorded nearly every happening in the Regiment's life, describes the event.

Presentation and Consecration of Colour

On the 2nd March, 1921, the Silk Union Flag presented by His Majesty the King to the 11th (Service) - Donegal and Fermanagh - Battalion, Royal Inniskilling Fusiliers, was brought from Omagh to Enniskillen by a small Colour escort from the Regimental Depot. under the command of Major C. A. M. Alexander, M.C., the Colour being carried by Lieut. F. W. Martin, M.C.

Enniskillen was en fete for the occasion, Union Jacks were displayed in the windows, National emblems floated from the various public buildings, and bunting was everywhere in profusion.

The place of assembly was the Square, Main Barracks, where the troops of the Garrison were on parade. The 9th (Queen's Royal) Lancers were formed up on three sides of the square. Facing the 9th Lancers was a Guard of Honour of the Ulster Special Constabulary, comprised of men who had served in the Inniskillings. The Guard looked exceptionally well in their new police uniforms, their many decorations showing up brightly on their dark uniform. In the rear of the Guard of Honour the ex-soldiers of the 11th Battalion were formed up, under the command of Major C. F. Falls. The splendid band of the 1st Battalion Bedfordshire and Hertfordshire Regiment (bandmaster, J. E. S. Vince), kindly lent for the ceremony by Lieut. Colonel E. I. de S. Thorpe, D.S.O., was also on parade. On the square, outside the formation of the troops, many spectators had gathered.

The General Salute heralded the arrival of Brigadier-General A. St. Q. Ricardo, C.M.G., C.B.E., D.S.O.

General Ricardo then presented medals to various soldiers of the Garrison. The Distinguished Conduct Medal awarded to the late Sergt. I. Bates, 1st Battalion The Royal Inniskilling Fusiliers, was presented to his mother, to whom the General expressed his sympathy on the loss of such a gallant son.

The Colour escort advanced and the Colour being uncased, the Royal Salute was given, a trumpeter sounding a fanfare.

General Ricardo handed the Colour to Captain W. M. Knight, commanding the Guard of Honour, who received it on behalf of Lieut. Col. J. E. Knott, C.M.G., D.S.O., late Commanding Officer of the 11th Battalion.

Addressing the Inniskillings present Brig. Gen. Ricardo said that it was a great honour and privilege to him to hand to them the Colour that had been presented to them by His Majesty the King. The Colour had never been carried at the head of their Battalion, but the Colour was a symbol of what they had fought for, and for what so many of their comrades had died for. They had never let the Colour down, and they were now going to take it and put it alongside the colours of the Battalions of that splendid Regiment that both he and they belonged to - The Royal Inniskilling Fusiliers.

Colonel Knott thanked General Ricardo on behalf of the officers and men for having presented the colours. It was, he said, particularly suitable, that General Ricardo should perform this ceremony for he had been so long associated with the regiment in other Battalions, the 1st, the 9th, and later as General Officer Commanding the 109th Infantry Brigade. They were very sorry that General Hessey, the father of their Battalion, was from family reasons prevented from being with them. He took that, the first public opportunity of thanking the good people of counties Donegal and Fermanagh for their constant thought and care of their own Battalion. In this connection he would like to thank Mr. Trimble, and many others, including Mrs. Hessey who had been indefatigable in collecting the comforts and sending them out to those on service. He also thanked the Commanding Officer of the 9th Lancers and the Officer Commanding at the Depot for sending the Colour Party. He would like to congratulate the officer commanding the Lancers on his splendid body of men, and also the Bedfords for their fine band. He again thanked General Ricardo for handing them the colours which they kept at the Somme, Wytschaete, Ypres, and at Cambrai, unsullied.

Colonel Knott then called for three cheers for Colonel Ricardo, which were heartily given.

The ceremony having concluded, the Colour and escort marched to the Parish Church, headed by the band.

The Parish Church was crowded, and as the Colour was borne up the aisle the band played O'Hara's "The Perfect Melody." Halting at the foot of the chancel, the Guard of Honour stood down the aisle, with arms at the slope and bayonets fixed.

The short service of consecration was conducted by Right. Rev. Dr. Day, Bishop of Clogher.

Colonel Knott, the Commanding Officer of the Battalion, asked the Archdeacon and churchwardens to keep the Colour in a sacred place. He knew the parish would cherish it in honour of the gallant Battalion, and in memory of their brave fallen comrades. He hoped the Colour would always be an inspiration to those who would come afterwards, remembering the deeds done by the men of this Battalion.

The Colour was then handed over, the Guard presenting arms, and Archdeacon M'Manaway formally, on behalf of the parish, received the Colour and placed it on the communion table.

Brigadier General Ricardo, addressing the assembled congregation, said -

I look on it as a great honour to be asked to take part in this ceremony.

As an old Inniskillinger, I am glad to be afforded the opportunity of paying my tribute of admiration for the 11th Battalion Royal Inniskilling Fusiliers. We are here to hand into the keeping of your beautiful church - in the town which gave the Inniskillings their name - yet one more Colour of an Inniskilling Battalion. Some Battalions whose colours rest in this Church, have a history going back for several centuries. The Battalion, whose Colour is to take its place of honour today with these other revered flags, had a history brief in length of time compared with those of the line Battalions - but into its short life was crowded a very glorious record - and the King's Colour of the 11th Inniskillings is indeed worthy to take its place, side by side, with those of its parent Battalions. The 11th Battalion added many splendid pages to the history of the Regiment. I served side by side with the 11th during its entire career - for the first year I watched it training and imbibing the true Inniskilling spirit, under that incomparable Inniskilling soldier, General Hessey - and I can say no more than that. I always held up the 11th as an example and inspiration to my own Battalion. That is, believe me, a high tribute for every keen soldier thinks his Battalion is second to none, but I always found something to learn from General Hessey's Battalion. Then at the front for another year, when my Battalion had the 11th beside it, I never had any anxiety about our flank; if it was in support of us we were sure of help if needed; if in front of us we knew we would never have to retreat.

On the 1st July, 1916 that glorious, but dreadful day, the 11th were on the right of the line of the Ulster Division. Their flank was exposed to an overwhelming machine-gun fire, through no fault of their own. In spite of that the 11th gained their objective and covered themselves with imperishable glory. I saw their advance with my own eyes. I can never forget that scene - such quiet deliberate bravery was only possible in a Battalion with a tremendous pride in its Regiment; and with that perfect sympathy between its officers and men, which was always an outstanding characteristic of the 11th.

The next great action the Battalion was engaged in was at Wyteschaete on the Messine ridge in June, 1917, when I had the great honour of being their Brigadier. There the 11th led the Division on its left flank; along with the 16th Division the most complete success in one single day in the war up to date was the result to which the 11th Inniskillings contributed very considerably. Again it stood out as a fighting Battalion. Then east of Ypres, in August, 1917, at the beginning of that awful struggle for the Passchendaele ridge the 11th once more made history in getting further than any other unit in the Division. Then at Cambrai, in November, 1917, the third big fight inside six months, it helped to bomb the enemy out of the Hindenburg line, and then withstood their heavy counter attacks on the left flank.

Then came the time, when through no fault of their own, but solely on account of the casualties they had suffered they, together with many other Battalions were called upon to make a bitter sacrifice, they had to be broken up to fill other Battalions. But the surviving men and officers of the 11th took with them to their new unit the splendid traditions and spirit of their Battalion, and they fought on, again under General Hessey, until victory came at last. I have only touched on the larger actions in which the Battalion took part, but in addition to that for three years - winter and summer - the 11th faced the enemy in the trenches, and they never lost a yard of trench; they never let down another unit; they never failed their commander.

This brief testimony from one who knew them intimately, is no formal expression of opinion, nor spoken just to please you their friends - it is my considered judgment as a soldier - but one which as a close comrade, gives me heartfelt satisfaction to be able to state here today.

This Colour the King's Colour, they hand you here today was never carried at the head of their Battalion, but it was the flag under which they fought and for which so many of their dear comrades died. They never failed their King and country, they added tribute to the honours of that Regiment, second to none, to which you and I belong, and which bears the proud name of your town. What better resting place could there be than in this ancient church?

After the ceremony over one hundred and sixty officers and men of the 11th Battalion, the Colour escort from Depot and the band were entertained by the Fermanagh U.V.F. in the Protestant Hall, where a very excellent luncheon was provided. A number of ladies who were identified with the different military recreation rooms in Enniskillen during the war, kindly acted as attendants.

Mr. E. Archdale, M.P., presided at the luncheon. Excellent speeches were delivered by Mr. Archdale, General Ricardo, Colonel Knott, Major Falls, Major Moore, Major Myles, and Mr. Copeland Trimble, who has always been a good friend of the Inniskillings, and who, during the war, was instrumental in sending out large consignments of comforts to the Battalions overseas.

For some time past a small committee comprising Major C. F. Falls, Captain H. C. Gordon, M. C., Mr. S. C. Clarke, together with Lieut. Col. W. R. H. Dann, D.S.O., Commanding Enniskillen Garrison, and Ven. Archdeacon M'Manaway, with one or two others, had been making arrangements for the occasion and the result of their carefully thought out and capably executed plans was that everything passed off without the slightest hitch.

Then in December 1957 the colours of the Donegal Regiment of the Ulster Volunteers so faithfully preserved by Capt. Curley M.C. were handed over by a group of veterans to St. McCartin's Cathedral.

This event was organised by Mr. Bill Maxwell who for many years was associated with the Old Comrades Association and a friend of Capt. Curley M.C.

It seemed fitting the group was twenty seven in number. The Colour Party was commanded by Mr. S. Bullock M.C.

The standard bearers were Mr. A. McMullen M.M., a native of Ballyshannon, who was in the old South Donegal U.V.F., and Mr. J. J. McFarland M.M., Enniskillen. The escorts were Messrs. W. Clendinning, M.M., Lisbellaw, and Frank McConnell, Enniskillen, and accompanying them Mr. W. J. R. Maxwell, Hon Secretary of the Fermanagh Association in Belfast, who was responsible for all the arrangements.

The Colour party was met at the chancel steps by the Rector, who was accompanied by the churchwardens, Messrs. Albert D. Connolly and Walter Quinn.

Addressing the Rector, Mr. Bullock said - "These are the Colours of the Donegal Regiment of the Ulster Volunteer Force.

They are symbols of faith and patriotic service.

It is our desire that they should be placed here as permanent memorials. We ask you and the wardens of this Cathedral to accept them for safe keeping."

Canon Clements replied: "This we gladly do. We accept these Colours and shall have them placed upon the walls of this Cathedral as permanent memorials and dedicate them in the name of the Father, Son and Holy Ghost. Amen."

He then took the Colours and handed them to the churchwardens who placed one on each side of the Holy Table.

In the course of an address afterwards, Canon Clements said: "We have just now received the Colours of the Donegal Regiment of the Ulster Volunteer Force into the Cathedral. We have accepted them and have dedicated them for safe keeping on the walls of the Cathedral here, where they will always remind us of things which happened before many of us were born.

They will remind us of the watchfulness of men who were alert to the challenge of their age. They will remind us of men who acted decisively when the need arose."

Canon Clements said they were happy to have with them that morning some of the men who were closely associated with the personalities and events of those days.

Those, said Canon Clements, were critical days for their people and the existence of the Volunteer Force only emphasised to them the determination of the people to deal courageously and to deal realistically with what was a crisis.

It was a crisis not in a sense of a disaster, but in the sense of being a turning point - a time for decision. It was a crisis of a particularly definite and clear character. It was a time, one of those historical occasions, when a man's line of duty seemed to be very clear, "and," said Canon Clements, "the very existence of these Colours which we have just now received speaks to our imaginations the idea of men mustering in little and in large numbers in order to prepare for any struggle which might become necessary."

These Colours escaped being destroyed in an accidental fire in the Cathedral in March 1996.

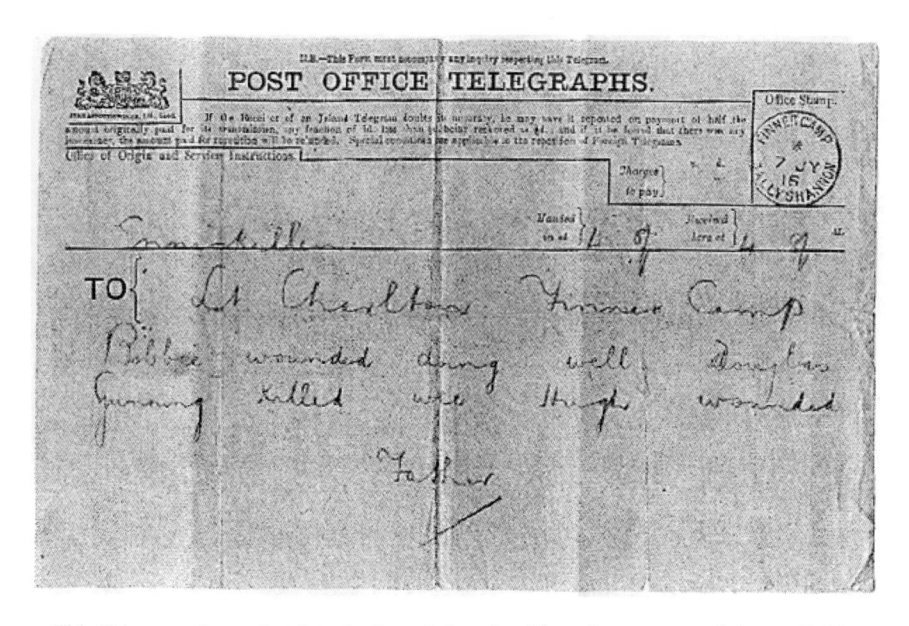

This Telegram shows that it took about 6 days for this sad news to reach home. Bobby was Lt. J.W. Charlton's brother. Hugh cannot be identified.

Above: Wytschaete after the battle

Left: Arthur McIlfatrick

Decorations Won by the Eleventh

This list has been prepared from all the information available to the writer. If there are any omissions or discrepancies I apologise.

2nd. Lt.	Adams, T.	M.C. and Bar
Capt.	Charlton, J. W.	M.C. and Bar Croix de Guerre
Capt.	Crosbie, D. E. R.A.M.C.	M.C.
Capt.	Curley, J.	M.C. Croix de Guerre avec Palmes
2nd. Lt.	Drean, R. S.	M.C.
Capt.	Falls, C. B.	Croix de Guerre
Capt.	Forde, G. M.	M.C. and Bar
Capt.	Gallaugher, H.	D.S.O.
2nd. Lt.	Ganly, R.	M.C.
Capt.	Gordon, H. C.	M.C. Belgian Order of Leopold
Capt.	Irvine, G. M. F.	M.C.
Capt.	Knight, W. M.	M.C. and Bar
Capt.	Moore, W.	M.C.
Capt.	Myles, J. S.	M.C.
Lt. Col.	Pratt	D.S.O.
Capt. Rev.	Spence, A. Chaplain	M.C.
2nd. Lt.	Strong, C. A.	M.C.
2nd. Lt.	Sweeny, T. C.	M.C.
T 2nd. Lt.	Talbot, Richard Hewitt	M.C.

L/Cpl.	Arkless, B.	M.M.
Sgt.	Armstrong, R.	M.M.
Cpl.	Barnhill, David	M.M.
Pte.	Beatty, J. R	M.M.
Sgt.	Blakey, David Harkness	M.M.
R.S.M.	Bleakley, Guy	M.C.
C.S.M.	Bullock, S	M.C.
Sgt.	Cairns, T.	M.M.
Cpl.	Clarke, J.	M.M.
Pte.	Connor, A.	M.M.
Sgt.	Dick, George	M.M.
Pte.	Donnell, S.	M.M.
L/Cpl.	Eames, W.	M.M.
Cpl.	Edwards, J.	M.M. and Bar

L/Cpl.	Elliott, W.	M.M.
Cpl.	Fawkes, F.	M.M.
Pte.	Ferguson, W. K.	M.M.
L.Cpl.	Fern, Harry	M.M.
Sgt.	Gardner, W.A.	M.M.
Pte.	Glenn, D.	Croix de Guerre
Pte.	Godfrey, E.	M.M.
Sgt.	Greaves, J.	M.M.
L/Cpl.	Gregory, C. H.	M.M.
Pte.	Haslett, L	D.C.M.
Sgt.	Hislop, S.	M.M.
L/Cpl.	Hogg, George Matthew	M.M.
Pte.	Hughes, J. F.	M.M.
Sgt.	Hunter, J.	D.C.M. M.M. Medal of St. George -3rd class (Russia)
Cpl.	Johnston, S.	M.M.
Pte.	Keys, T.	M.M.
Sgt.	Kirkpatrick	Croix de Guerre
C.S.M.	Laird, W.	M.M. and Bar Medaille Militaire
Pte.	H. Law	M.M.
Pte.	McCartney, H.	M.M.
L/Cpl.	McClintock, T.	M.M.
Pte.	McConnell, J.	M.M.
Pte.	McGhee, P.	M.M.
L/Cpl.	McIlwaine, J.	M.M.
L/Cpl.	McMullen, A.	M.M.
Pte.	Meeke, J.	M.M.
Pte.	Megahey, R.	M.M. and Bar
L/Cpl.	Muir, W.	M.M.
Sgt.	Murray, R.	M.M.
Pte.	Neill, R.	M.M.
Sgt.	Nesbitt, A.	M.M.
Sgt.	O'Hara, J.	M.M.
Pte.	Orgill, F.	M.M.
Pte.	Owens, W.	M.S.M.
Sgt.	Parke, James	M.M.
Sgt.	Porterfield, A.	Croix de Guerre
Cpl.	Reilly, J.	D.C.M.
Sgt.	Roulston, R.	M.M.
L/Cpl.	Rutledge, William George	M.M.
Cpl.	Stitt, J.	M.M.

Pte.	Sweeney, J.	M.M.
Pte.	Taylor, A.	M.M.
Pte.	Tisseman, J.	M.M.
Pte.	Tulip, J. O.	M.M.
Sgt.	Warren, J.	M.M.
C.Q.M.S.	Woods, John	D.C.M.
Pte.	Wray, Charles	M.M.

Abbreviations
D.S.O.   Distinguished Service Order
M.C.   Military Cross
D.C.M.   Distinguished Conduct Medal
M.M.   Military Medal
M.S.M.   Meritorious Service Medal

Roll of Honour

11th Battalion

Ackerman, T.	Inmarsh, Gloucester
Adair, J.	Omagh, Co. Tyrone
Allan, W.	South Shields, Durham
Allen, A.	Enniskillen, Co Fermanagh
Anders, J.	Newcastle-on-Tyne, Durham
Anderson, C.	Wallsend-on-Tyne, Durham
Anderson, J.	Ballinamallard, Co. Fermanagh
Anderson, James	Belfast, Co. Antrim
Anderson, R.	Dungannon, Co. Tyrone
Archibald, D.	Glasgow
Armstrong, A.	Trillick, Co. Tyrone
Armstrong, J.	Newtownbutler, Co. Fermanagh
Arthur, D.	Glasgow
Asbury, A.	Pimlico, London
Atkinson, G.	Gateshead, Durham
Atkinson, J.	Wrekenton, Durham
Aukland, C.	Gateshead, Durham
Averill, J.	Hebburn-on-Tyne, Durham
Baird, J.	Clonleigh, Co. Donegal
Ballintine, Joseph Capt.	Londonderry
Balmer, F.	High Spew, Durham
Barber, H.	Battersea, Surrey
Barclay, R.	Montrose, Forfar
Bargh, F.	Sheffield, Yorkshire
Barlow, J.	Reading, Berkshire
Barnhill, D.	Ballylawn, Co. Donegal
Barr, P.	Londonderry, Co. Derry
Barrow, J.	South Shields, Durham
Beattie, J.	Raphoe, Co. Donegal
Beattie, John James	Hillsborough, Co. Down
Beatty, W.	Tempo, Co. Fermanagh
Bell, D.	Gateshead, Durham
Bennett, H.	Helland, Gloucester
Bennett, J.	Ballygowan, Co. Down
Beresford, A.	Gateshead, Durham
Bird, F.	Innismacsaint, Co. Fermanagh

Blackwood, W.	Ballymacarrett, Co. Down
Blakey, D.	Felling, Durham
Bloxham, W.	West Bromwich, Staffordshire
Bodle, G.	Knackbride, Co. Donegal
Bogle, W.	Mount Charles, Co. Donegal
Bonner, J.	Templemore, Co. Derry
Booth, A.	Co. Derry
Bowes, J.	Aughavea, Co. Fermanagh
Brabrooke, W.	Bury St. Edmunds
Bradley, D.	Desertagney, Co. Donegal
Bradley, G.	Raphoe, Co. Donegal
Bradley, J.	Craighadoes, Co. Donegal
Brooks, J.	Openshaw, Durham
Brown, C.	Newcastle-on-Tyne, Durham
Brown, W.	Aghavea, Co. Fermanagh
Brown, Walter	Usworth, Durham
Bryans, R.	Lisnaskea, Co. Fermanagh
Buchanan, S.	Burt, Co. Donegal
Burns, J.	Calton, Glasgow
Burns, R.	Bailieboro, Co. Cavan
Burrell, G.	Northfleet, Hants.
Byrne, J.	Tinahely, Co. Wicklow
Campbell, J.	Barony, Lanark
Campbell, R.	Glasgow
Campbell, Robert A.	Connor, Co. Antrim
Carlile, Thomas 2nd. Lt.	
Carroll, W.	Seaham, Durham
Carrothers, J.	Tempo, Co. Fermanagh
Cary, R.	Liverpool, Lancs.
Cathcart, R.	Ramelton, Co. Donegal
Cathers, A.	Magheraculmoney, Co. Fermanagh
Chambers, J.	Cavan
Chambers, W.	Salford, Manchester
Chaters, J.	Colliery, Durham
Cherry, J.	Lisburn, Co. Antrim
Chesnutt, R.	Kilcarr, Co. Donegal
Chesnutt, T.	Killybegs, Co. Donegal
Clark, J.	Chislehurst, Kent
Clark, John Thomas	Nottingham, N. Hants.
Clarke, G.	Ballintra, Co. Donegal
Clarke, W.	Glasgow

Clements, T.	Churchtown, Co. Donegal
Clements, Thomas Lipton 2nd. Lt.	Dublin Road, Omagh
Clements, W.	Ballymacarrett, Co. Down
Clements, Wm. Hunter M.S.M. 2nd. Lt.	Cliftonville, Belfast
Coalter, W.	Limehouse, Middlesex
Coleman, T.	Shankhill, Co. Antrim
Colgate, J.	Ilford, Essex
Colhoun, G.	Donaghmore, Co. Donegal
Collins, R.	Ballymacarrett, Co. Down
Colvin, J.	Glasgow
Copley, A.	Hammersmith, Middlesex
Cousins, V.	Kinawley, Co. Fermanagh
Coventry, J.	Castlefin, Co. Donegal
Craig, John Arnott Taylor 2nd. Lt.	Co. Down
Craig, W.	Culmore, Co. Derry
Cranston, W.	Lisbellaw, Co. Fermanagh
Craven, J.	Hebburn-on-Tyne, Durham
Crawford, H.	Kinawley, Co. Fermanagh
Crawford, R.	Swanlinbar, Co. Fermanagh
Crease, L.	St. Silas, Bristol
Crockett, J.	Ballymaclenaghan, Co. Derry
Crommer, R.	Killymard, Co. Donegal
Cullen, R.	Killasnet, Manorhamilton, Co. Letrim
Dale, T.	Garvagh, Co. Derry
Dandy, R.	Hebburn, Durham
Dane, W.	Benmore, Co. Fermanagh
Davidson, W.	St. Anne's, Belfast
Davison, T.	Newcastle-on-Tyne
Dawson, S.	Portglenone, Co. Derry
Deasley, W.	Callon, Co. Donegal
Dempsey, H.	Glasgow
Devenny, W.	Ray, Co. Donegal
Devers, R.	Willowfield, Co. Antrim
Diamond, J.	Dailly, Ayrshire
Dinsmore, J.	Carnmoyle, Co. Donegal
Dinsmore, R.	Culmore, Co. Derry
Diss, W.	Deptford, Middlesex
Dixon, T.	Maryport, Cumberland
Dogherty, D.	Letterkenny, Co. Donegal
Dogherty, J.	Letterkenny, Co. Donegal
Donaghey, W.	Garshuey, Co. Donegal

Dornan, T.	Ballynafeigh, Co. Down
Downey, G.	Lallaghey, Co. Fermanagh
Draper, W.	Leeds, Yorkshire
Drew, F.	Orchard Bishop, Co. Down
Drury, L.	Matlock, Derby
Dunn, A.	Castletown, Co. Donegal
Dunn, R.	Cramlington, Northumberland
Eames, H.	Rossony, Enniskillen
Easter, G.	Gateshead, Durham
Elliott, T.	Kaillesher, Co. Fermanagh
Elliott, W.	Wellington Quay, Northumberland
Elsbury, E.	Oakenshaw, Durham
Evers, J.	Silksworth, Durham
Fairbrother, J.	Liverpool, Lancs.
Fairbrother, S.	Liverpool, Lancs.
Fenwick, J.	Newcastle-on-Tyne, Durham
Fern, H.	Gruntleford, Derby
Ferron, S.	Dublin
Fifield, J.	Woodgreen, Middlesex
Finnegan, J.	Newcastle-on-Tyne, Durham
Finnegan, R.	Westgate, Newcastle-on-Tyne
Finney, W.	Ilkeston, Derby
Fleming, T.	Convoy, Co. Donegal
Fluke, Samuel Capt.	
Foster, F.	Wardley Colliery, Durham
Foster, J.	Kilmainham, Ballinagh, Co. Cavan
Furness, J.	Crook, Durham
Galbraith, A.	Donegal
Galbraith, J.	Binion, Co. Donegal
Galbraith, John	Drumcrow, Co. Donegal
Gallagher, C.	Minnervalley, Co. Donegal
Gallaugher, Henry D.S.O. Capt.	Manorcunningham, Co. Donegal
Gallon, W.	Swalwell, Durham
Garbett, J.	Dukinfield, Lancs.
Gardiner, A.	Greenock, Renfrew
Gardiner, S.	Enniskillen, Co. Fermanagh
Gardner, P.	Glasgow
Gibson, J.	Maryhill, Glasgow
Gibson, R.	Raphoe, Co. Donegal
Gilchrist, J.	Burt, Co. Donegal
Gill, W.	Greenside, Durham

Gilmore, W.	Killea, Co. Donegal
Girvan, H.	Anderston, Glasgow
Goldsmith, M.	Newcastle-on-Tyne, Durham
Gordon, R.	Windsor Avenue, Belfast
Gourley, J.	Raphoe, Co. Donegal
Gowans, D.	Dalbetten, Kircudbrightshire
Graham, B.	Pettigo, Co. Donegal
Graham, J.	Templecarn, Co. Fermanagh
Graham, James	Killymard, Co. Donegal
Graham, John	Tinoley, Co. Fermanagh
Green, T.	Glasgow
Gregory, J.	Ballybofey, Co. Donegal
Grindle, W.	Clones, Co. Monaghan
Gunning, Frank Douglas 2nd. Lt.	Enniskillen, Co. Fermanagh
Hagan, T.	Drummand, Co. Tyrone
Hall, C.	Portsmouth, Hants.
Hall, J.	Lewisham, Middlesex
Hamilton, John 2nd. Lt.	Ballymoney, Co. Antrim
Hammond, W.	Castledawson, Co. Derry
Harding, M.	Washington, Durham
Hargreaves, T.	Blackroll, Chorley, Lancs.
Harrison, J.	Moate, Co. Westmeath
Harrison, Samuel Dunlop Henderson Lt.	
Hawksworth, T.	Melbourne, Derby
Hayton, T.	Usworth, Durham
Heaney, A.	Drumachose, Limavady, Co. Derry
Henderson, R.	Carlisle, Cumberland
Henderson, W.	Glasgow
Hennessy, W.	Kilcoman, Co. Wicklow
Hepburn, S.	Ferry Hill, Durham
Heslip, H.	Newcastle, Co. Down
Hobrough, S.	Notting Hill, Middlesex
Hogg, G.	Dunfanaghy, Co. Donegal
Holahan, T.	St. Thomas, Dublin
Hollawell, T.	Lisbellaw, Co. Fermanagh
Holmes, J.	Ballymacarrett, Co.Down
Holmes, James	Donaghmore, Co. Donegal
Holmes, W.	Donemana, Co. Tyrone
House, H.	Swerston, Notts.
Hoye, G.	Enniskillen, Co. Fermanagh
Hunt, A.	Cheltenham

Hunter, G.	Glasgow
Hunter, W.	Tandragee, Co. Armagh
Hunter, William	Wrekenton, Durham
Hutchinson, J.	Scotswood, Durham
Inglas, J.	Kirkaldy, Fife
Irvine, D.	Pettigo, Co. Donegal
Irvine, J.	Granton, Midlothian
Irvine, James	Enniskillen, Co. Fermanagh
Irvine, S.	Shankhill, Co. Antrim
Irving, J.	North Shields, Durham
Johnston, A.	Wellingham, Notts.
Johnston, Angus	Kingston, Lanark
Johnston, D.	Derryhaney, Co. Fermanagh
Johnston, H.	Glasgow
Johnston, W.	Glasgow
Johnston, William	Boho, Co. Fermanagh
Jones, T.	Bala, North Wales
Kelly, J.	Newcastle-on-Tyne, Durham
Kennedy, J.	Shankhill, Co. Antrim
Kennedy, James	Glasgow
Kennedy, James Joseph Lt.	Dublin
Kenny, M.	Aughabeagh, Co. Fermanagh
Kerr, M.	Newcastle-on-Tyne, Durham
Kerr, R.	Tempo, Co. Fermanagh
Kerr, T.	Innishmacart, Co. Fermanagh
Kerrigan, J.	Kilclean, Co. Donegal
Keys, J.	Muff, Co. Donegal
Kilpatrick, W.	Innismacsaint, Co. Fermanagh
Kinkaid, W.	Taughboyne, Co. Donegal
Kinnaird, D.	Reyswood, Northumberland
Kirkpatrick, A.	Ballymoney, Co. Antrim
Knight, T.	Ballydoolagh, Co. Fermanagh
Kyle, G.	Sherburn, Durham
Kyle, J.	Greenock, Renfrew
Laird, C.	Kilbarron, Co. Donegal
Lanigan, W.	Clondalkin, Co. Dublin
Larmouth, G.	Sacriston, Durham
Leslie, R.	St. Nicholas, Cork
Lindsay, A.	Clonlee, Co. Donegal
Lindsay, J.	Derrybrush, Co. Fermanagh
Little, J.	Priory, Co. Fermanagh

Lockhart, A.	Kilatee, Co. Donegal
Logan, T.	Ardara, Co. Donegal
Long, F.	Kilatee, Co. Donegal
Lowes, N.	St. Andrews, Newcastle-on-Tyne
Lowry, M.	Glasgow
McCaffrey, W.	Rossory, Co. Fermanagh
McCaskill, A.	Durnish, Inverness
McCelland, J.	Lisnaskea, Co. Fermanagh
McClelland, S.	Ballymoney, Co. Antrim
McClintock, R.	Magheracoolmoney, Co. Tyrone
McClintock, W.	Muff, Co. Donegal
McCluskey, J.	Shankhill, Co. Antrim
McCluskey, S.	Parton, Cumberland
McComas, G.	Mountmellick, Queens Co.
McConkey, R.	Mullingar, Westmeath
McConnell, J.	Mahercross, Co. Fermanagh
McConnell, R.	Glasgow
McCourt, P.	Clones, Co. Monaghan
McCrea, W. J.	Foiden, Tempo, Co. Fermanagh
McCrory, H.	Shankhill, Co. Antrim
McCrum, A.	Shankhill, Co. Antrim
McCullagh, A.	Donaghmore, Co. Donegal
McCullagh, Alexander Henry 2nd. Lt.	Antrim Road, Belfast
McIlfatrick, S.	Tamlaght, Co. Derry
McFarland, A.	Ballindrait, Co. Donegal
McGhie, J.	Stewartstown, Co. Tyrone
McGirr, M.	Gallon, Co. Fermanagh
McGlinchey, J.	Fintona, Co. Tyrone
McGowan, E.	Burnhead Close, Falkirk
McGowan, J.	Casltethird, Co. Donegal
McGowan, R.	Dalmuir, Glasgow
McGrail, J.	Co. Fermanagh
McGuckin, J.	Ballinderry, Co. Derry
McIlroy, H.	Ballymena, Co. Antrim
McIntyre, C.	Whitehaven, Cumberland
McIntyre, J.	Templemore, Co. Derry
McKay, A.	Glasgow
McKelvey, J.	Omagh, Co. Tyrone
McKendrick, C.	Camus, Co. Tyrone
McKenzie, J.	Glasgow
McKenzie, S.	Enniskillen, Co. Fermanagh

McKeown, T.	Garraghey, Co. Tyrone
McKinlay, R.	Glendermott, Co. Derry
McLaughlin, J.	Cross, Co. Donegal
McLeer, W.	Fintona, Co. Tyrone
McLoughlin, B.	Limavady, Co. Derry
McMonagle, A.	Londonderry, Co. Derry
McQuade, J.	Aghavea, Co. Fermanagh
McQuillan, T.	Mullaghvoy, Co. Derry
Macbeth, W.	Monien, Co. Donegal
Macourt, H.	Irvinestown, Co. Fermanagh
Mann, R.	Ballymena, Co. Antrim
Manning, A.	Downpatrick, Co. Down
Marcus, T.	Glasgow
Marriott, G.	Prass, near Ashover, Derby
Marsh, J.	Newherrington, Durham
Matthews, B.	Shankhill, near Lurgan, Co. Armagh
Matthews, S.	Shankhill, Co. Antrim
Maxwell, G.	Glasgow
Mehaffy, T.	Castlefin, Co. Donegal
Middlemas, J.	Oakenshaw, Durham
Miller, G.	Barony, Lanark
Miller, Stanley 2nd. Lt.	Camberley, Surrey
Miller, T.	West Kilbride, Renfrew
Miller, W.	St. George's, London
Milligan, J.	Tullyrusher, Co. Tyrone
Milligan, W.	Ramelton, Co. Donegal
Mitchell, E.	Tiverton, Somerset
Moffitt, J.	Irvinestown, Co. Fermanagh
Montgomery, H.	Drumskew, Co. Fermanagh
Moon, W.	Gateshead, Durham
Moore, H.	Redlands, Gloucester
Morgan, W.	Consett, Durham
Morrison, A.	Glasgow
Morrison, J.	Aughalurcher, Co. Fermanagh
Morrison, W.	Blacklion, Co. Caven
Morrissy, J.	Gowran, Kilkenny
Morrow, G.	Clabby, Co. Fermanagh
Murdock, D.	Barnley, Lanark
Musgrove, J.	Sacriston, Durham
Nabney, W.	Ballymacarrett, Co. Down
Nassan, P.	Paddington, Middlesex

Nattras, S.	Sunnyside, Durham
Nelson, C.	Belfast, Co. Antrim
Nelson, J.	Upperlands, Co. Derry
Nelson, S.	Upperlands, Co. Derry
Newell, F.	High Wycombe, Bucks.
Newton, P.	Lochee, Dundee
Nicholls, H.	Bridgewater, Somerset
Nixon, W.	Enniskillen, Co. Fermanagh
Norwood, John Norton 2nd. Lt.	Glasgow
O'Conner, J.	St. Peter's, Antrim
Orr, L.	Templemore, Co. Derry
Orr, W.	Templemore, Co. Derry
Owens, R.	Armagh
Palmer, H.	Marylebone, Middlesex
Park, J.	Ballymena, Co. Antrim
Parke, J.	Moville, Co. Donegal
Parker, N.	Glasgow
Patrick, J.	Ballyhinney, Co. Antrim
Patterson, T.	Plahetts, Northumberland
Peak-Garland, George 2nd. Lt.	Avebury, Marlborough
Pearson, J.	Usworth, Durham
Peoples, G	Doacarrick, Co. Donegal
Peoples, George	Randalstown, Co. Antrim
Pinkerton, J.	Stranorlar, Co. Donegal
Porter, R.	Letterkenny, Co. Donegal
Porter, Reuben	Marylebone, Middlesex
Postlethwaite, J.	Ryhope, Durham
Potter, J.	Caledon, Co. Tyrone
Potter, W.	Charmouth, Dorset
Potts, A.	Shankhill, Co. Antrim
Potts, J.	Belfast, Co. Antrim
Pouncey, W.	Wigan, Lancs.
Pratt, Audley Charles D.S.O. Lt. Col.	Crossmolina, Co. Mayo
Pratt, J.	Newbottle, Durham
Queen, J.	Glasgow
Quinn, J.	Brackaville, Co. Tyrone
Quinton, H.	Ballindrait, Co. Donegal
Reid, J.	Finvoy, Co. Antrim
Reilly, R.	Enniskillen, Co. Fermanagh
Rentoul, J.	Cambuslang, Lanark
Reoche, H.	Kilbarron, Co. Donegal

Rexter, J.	Innismore, Co. Fermanagh
Rice, A.	Sedgletch, Durham
Richards, J.	Camberwell, Middlesex
Richards, W.	Wellington Quay, Northumberland
Richardson, T.	Ryhope, Durham
Richardson, Thomas Henry	Midgeholme, Cumberland
Ritchie, G.	Killymard, Co. Donegal
Rivenell, J.	Fulham, Middlesex
Robb, A.	Churchtown, Castlederg, Co. Tyrone
Robertson, J.	Glasgow
Robertson, John Gilfillan 2nd. Lt.	Camera House, Boyle, Co. Roscommon
Rose, G.	Enniskillen, Co. Fermanagh
Roulston, T.	Ballindrait, Co. Donegal
Rowe, T.	Aghalure, Co. Fermanagh
Rutherford, T.	Great Lumley, Durham
Rutledge, W.	Killargue, Co. Leitrim
Scarlett, J.	Drumhaghma, Co. Fermanagh
Scattergood, J.	Nottingham
Scott, A.	Drumconnor, Co. Donegal
Scott, Alexander	Shankhill, Co. Antrim
Scott, J.	Rathmullan, Co. Donegal
Seals, C.	Walthorps, Derby
Seed, T.	Spotley Bridge, Durham
Sewell, William Tait Capt.	Sunderland, Co. Durhan
Shaw, J.	Pettigo, Co. Donegal
Shaw, T.	Lisbellaw, Co. Fermanagh
Shirley, R.	Fintona, Co. Tyrone
Simpson, H.	Glasgow
Simpson, Henry	South Shields, Durham
Simpson, J.	Lisnaskea, Co. Fermanagh
Simpson, James	Aughavea, Co. Fermanagh
Simpson, P.	Philadelphia, U.S.A., Enlisted Enniskillen
Simpson, R.	Lisnaskea, Co. Fermanagh
Smith, A.	Raphoe, Co. Donegal
Smith, S.	Toome, Co. Antrim
Smith, T.	Gainsborough, Lincolnshire
Smith, W.	Houghton Gate, Durham
Smyth, E.	Raphoe, Co. Donegal
South, R.	Glasgow
Speer, A.	Letterkenny, Co. Donegal
Spence, G.	Kilmore, Co. Armagh

Spence, W.	Portstewart, Co. Derry
Spillane, J.	Mormeal, Co. Derry
Starr, Arthur James 2nd. Lt.	Newtownhamilton, Co. Armagh
Steenson, J.	Warrenpoint, Co. Down
Stephenson, N.	Gateshead, Durham
Stevenson, J.	Drumerdagh, Co. Donegal
Stevenson, T.	Killyman, Co. Tyrone
Stewart, H.	Irvinestown, Co. Fermanagh
Stewart, J.	Usworth, Durham
Stewart, T.	Keely, Co. Derry
Stewart, William McEwan Henderson 2nd. Lt.	
Stinson, J.	Derrygonnelly, Co. Fermanagh
Stone, J.	Sansley, Derby
Strafford, J.	New Lambton, Durham
Stratton, W.	Killyman, Co. Tyrone
Straughan, T.	Tynedock, Durham
Sutherland, D.	Glasgow
Swaddle, R.	Dunstan, Durham
Sweeney, A.	Templemore, Co. Derry
Sword, W.	Newcastle-on-Tyne
Symington, G.	Maguiresbridge, Co. Fermanagh
Taylor, R.	Killea, Co. Donegal
Thomas, E.	Barking, Essex
Thompson, F.	Maguiresbridge, Co. Fermanagh
Thompson, J.	Newcastle-on-Tyne
Thompson, S.	St. Alkmonds, Derby
Threadkill, W.	Enniskillen, Co. Fermanagh
Toland, S.	Tempo, Co. Fermanagh
Topp, Richard William 2nd. Lt.	Newry
Trainor, P.	Scotstown, Monaghan
Turner, S.	Nottingham
Twissel, G.	Nottingham
Vance, E.	Co. Fermanagh
Walker, J.	Castlelinden, Co. Tyrone
Walker, John Johnston	Enniskillen, Co. Fermanagh
Walker, T.	Worthenden, Cheshire
Walsh, C.	Whitehall, Westmeath
Wardle, R.	Gateshead, Durham
Watson, L.	Sudbury, Suffolk
Watson, R.	Callerton, Northumberland
Watson, S.	Convoy, Co. Donegal

Watson, W.	Convoy, Co. Donegal
Watts, W.	Edinburgh, Linlithgow
Weightman, H.	Newcastle-on-Tyne, Durham
Weir, R.	Derryharney, Co. Fermanagh
Weir, W.	Glasgow
Weston, H.	Barrow Hill, Derby
Whiston, C.	Hanley, Stafford
White, J.	Barony, Glasgow
White, James	Townhead, Glasgow
White, R.	Innismagrath, Drumkure, Co. Leitrim
Wiggins, J.	Derrybrusk, Co. Fermanagh
Wightman, T.	Newcastle-on-Tyne, Durham
Wilkinson, A.	Shildon, Durham
Wilkinson, J.	Marley Hill, Durham
Williams, G.	Mulray, Co. Donegal
Williamson, T.	Canary, Co. Armagh
Wilson, D.	Kesh, Co. Fermanagh
Wilson, J.	Glasgow
Wilson, R.	Newfields, Durham
Wilson, T.	Ebrington, Derry
Wilson, W.	Glasgow
Witherow, J.	Maryport, Cumberland
Woods, T.	Monkwearmouth, Durham
Woods, W.	Killadeas, Co. Fermanagh
Wray, C.	Taughboyne, Co. Donegal
Wray, J.	Donaghboyne, Co. Donegal
Wright, A.	Gateshead, Durham
Wright, W.	Lurgan, Co. Armagh
Wylie, J.	Thornley, Durham
Wylie, James	Glasgow
Wylie, T.	Ballywatermoy, Co. Antrim
Yielding, A.	Hastings, Sussex
Young, R.	Bailieboro, Co. Cavan
Young, T.	Meekley, Northumberland

Index

CHAPTER 1 -
An Early Memory

Buchanan, Stewart	1
Burt	1
Canning, Samuel	1
Connaught Rangers	1
Donegal	1
Donegal and Fermanagh Volunteers	1
Fermanagh	1
Ireland	2
Irishmen	2
Regimental History	1, 2
Somme	1
Ulster Volunteer	1

CHAPTER 2 -
The Ulster Volunteers in Donegal and Fermanagh

Aghnadrum	5
Ardara	10
Ballindrait	11
Ballinamallard	6
Ballindara	4
Ballintra	10
Ballylennon	11
Ballymagroarty	10
Ballynakillen	10
Ballyshannon	10
Belfast	6
Belleek	6, 9
Blaney	5
Boers	3, 4
Brookeborough	4, 5
Bullock, Steve	12
Burt	11

Carson MP, Sir Edward	3, 4
Castle Hume	7
Castle Irvine	5, 6
Castlefin	11
Cavan	4
Cecil MP, Sir Hugh	4
Clara	10
Clarke, S.C.	7
Clonelly	5
Clones	8
Co. Monaghan	4, 8
Convoy	11
Crawford, John	8, 10
Crom	5
Crosbie, Dr.	11
Culley	10
Davidson D.S.O., Col.	4
Derrygonnelly	6
Derrygore	6
Derrylin	4
Devers, Robert	8
Donegal	4, 10, 11
Donegal Regiment	11
Donoughmore	11
Doran, Lieut, Col.	8
Dunlop, John	8
Earl of Erne	8
Earl of Lanesborough	6
Egerton D.S.O., Capt. Arthur	7
Enniskillen	5, 7
Ervine, Thomas	10
Falls, Chas F.	6
Fermanagh	5, 6
Fermanagh Regiment	6, 7
Finner Camp	3
Florencecourt	4, 5
Garrison	9
Greenhill	4

156

Hackett-Payne, Col.	7, 11	St. Johnston	11
Henry, George	10	Stack, Mr. M. T.	4
Hilltown	10	Stack, Rev. W.	4
Home Rule Bill	3	Tempo	5
Impartial Reporter	4	Topped Mountain	6
Inver	10	Unionists	9
Irvine, Major D'Arcy	4	Viscount Crighton D.S.O.	6
Irvinestown	6	Wagentreiber, W.H.	11
Johnston, James	10	Wilson, Rev. J.O.	8
Kesh	4, 6	Wray, James	10
Killatee	10		
Killynard	10		
Kinawley	4, 5	**CHAPTER 3 -**	
Kirk, Joseph	10	**War is Declared**	
Knockballymore	8		
Laghey	10	Austro-Hungary	13
League and Covenant	4	Belgium	13
Letterbreen	4	Britain	13
Letterkenny	11	Carson	13
Lisbellaw	5	Colours	13
Lisnaskea	4, 5	Craig	13
Lord Leitrim	11	Earl of Leitrim	13
Madden, Major	9	Ferdinand, Archduke Francis	13
Maguiresbridge	4, 5	France	13
Manorcunningham	11	Germany	13
McCourt, Robert	8	Hickman, Col.	13
Moyne	10	Hobsons of London	13
Myles JP, J. Sproule	10, 11	Irish Volunteers	14
Nationalists	4, 9	Lord Kitchener	13
Newtownbutler	5	Loyalists	14
Orange Order	3	National Volunteers	14
Pettigo	6, 9	Nationalists	14
Pierce, Charles	8	Redmond	14
Pine-Coffin, Major	11	Russia	13
Raphoe	11	Sarajevo	13
Rathmelton	11		
Ray	11		
Richardson, Gen. Sir George	5, 7	**CHAPTER 4 -**	
Rosnowlagh	10	**The Donegal Regiment**	
Ross JP, Charles	10		
Rosslea	4	Ballintine, J.	19

Ballyshannon	17, 18	Myles, J.S.	19
Bleakley, R.S.M.	16	Omagh	15
Boer War Camp	15	Quigley, Pte. James	17
Boynton, J.G.	19	Reid, A.S.C.	18
Bundoran	17, 18	Roulston, Pte. Robert	15
Burt	19	Royal Barracks	18
Butler, H.C.	19	Scotland	19
Canon Naylor	17	Shane's Castle	17
Carnamaddy	19	South Africa	15, 16
Castle Barracks	18	St. Johnston	17
Churchill, Winston	16	Transvaal	16
Colenso	16	Tugela Heights	16
County Antrim	17	Vaal Krantz	16
Craig, J.A.T.	19	Wagentreiber, W.H.	19
Crosbie RAMC, Lt. Douglas E.	18	Wallace, Joe	19
Dixie	19	Williamson, W.R.	19
Donegal	15		
Durham University OTC	16		
Falls, C.B.	17, 19	**CHAPTER 5 -**	
Falls, C.F.	19	**Changing Times**	
Fegan, Col.	18		
Fermanagh	15, 17	Belfast	20, 21
Finner Camp	15, 18, 19	Chelsea Barracks	20
Gilliland, G.F.	19	Dublin	21
Gordon, H.C.	19	Elliot, Serg. T.	20, 21
Hart, A.C.	19	Falls, Lt. C.B.	21
Hessey, Lt. Col. William	15, 19	Fitzgerald, Major W.	21
Hildebrand, Inspector	18	Forde, G.M.	21
Inniskilling Hill	16	Gallaugher, Lt. H.	20
Ladysmith	16	Hamilton, Serg. J.	20
Lord Leitrim	16, 19	Hessey, Lt. Col.	20
Lough Swilly	18	Iliffe, Sgt. W.	21
Lydenberg	16	Irwin, Capt. G.R.	21
MacKenzie, Major	16	London Gazette	21
McCorkell, B.F.	19	Lord Leitrim	20
McGuire	18	Mater Hospital	21
McIldowie, J.D.	19	McConkey, Sgt. E.	20
McIntyre, L.W.	19	McConley, Sgt. R.	21
Moore, Capt. R.L.	16, 19	McCorkell, B.F.	21
Moore, W.	19	Moore, Capt. R.L.	20
Munn, E.M.	19	Munn, E.M.	21

Munn, Lt. L.	20
Newcastle Upon Tyne	20
Olphert, G.	20
Omagh	20
Orr, R.G.	21
Randalstown	20
Roulston, Corp. J.	20
Rowe, Pte. Thomas	21
Shane's Castle	20
Smart, C/Sgt.	21
Stewart, Serg. J. Bryan	21
Webb, G.H.	21
Williamson, T.	20

CHAPTER 6 - Enthusiasm and Inspections

Arkless, Pte.	25
Ballintine, Lt. J.	22
County Antrim	22
Crosbie RAMC, Lt. D.E.	25
Falls, Lt. C.B.	22
Gallaugher, Lt.	25
General Friend	22
Hart, Lt. J.	22
Hessey, Lt. Col.	22
Hickman C.B.E. DSO, Brigadier T.E.	22, 25
Knight, Lt. W.	25
Lady Wimborne	23
Lord Leitrim	25
McCourt, Sgt.	22
Quigley, James	23
Randalstown	23
Ridge Camp	23
Sewell, Capt.	25
Shane's Castle	23
St. Johnston	23
Viceroy Lord Wimborne	23
Whittle, Cpl.	22
Williamson, Cpl.	22

CHAPTER 7 - Further Preparations

Bleakley, R.Q.M.S. J.	26
Bramshott	28
Carson, Sir Edward	28
Dublin	26, 27
Falls, C.B.	27
Falls, Major	27
Finner Camp	26
G. Murray, Lt. Gen. Sir A.	27
Gallaugher, H.	27
Hanna, Lt. J.R.M.	27
Italian Veterli	28
Kitchener K.P., Field Marshal Lord	28
Lord Leitrim	27
McCrea, Lt. T.	28
Moore, Major	27
Reid, Lt. J.A.	27
Seaford	27
Sussex	27
Trimble, W.	26
Turner, David	26

CHAPTER 8 - On to France

Boulougne	30
Bramshott	30
Cardonette	30, 31
Condas	31
Donegal	31
Fermanagh	31
Flesselles	30, 31
Hamel	31
Havre	30
Hedauville	31
Impartial Reporter	32
Liphook	30
Monro KCB, Gen. Sir C.C.	30

Montgomery, Pte.	31	**CHAPTER 11 -**	
Ostrohove	30	**Distinguished Conduct**	
Pouchevillers	31		
Southampton	30	Beaumont Hamel	41
Surrey	30	Boche	44, 46, 51
		Boyton, Capt. J.	42
		Brotherstone, Pte. T.	42
CHAPTER 9 -		Brown, Pte. E.	42
Infantry Weather		Campbell, Pte. A.	42
		Clarke, L/Cpl. G.	42
Aisne	34	Devine Pte. A.	42
Brucamps	35	Dolly's Brae	49
Candas	35	Falls, Second Lieut. Cyril	43
Christmas Day	36	Forceville	41
Donegal	34	Gabutt, Pte.	42
Fermanagh	34	Gallaugher, Henry	51
Hedauville	34	Glasgow	42
Hessey, Lt. Col. W.F.	36	Hamel	42
Hickman, Brig. J.	36	Hazlett, Pte. Louis	41, 51
Lord Leitrim	36	Hicks, Pte. T.	42
Mons	34	Jacob's Ladder	42
		Johnston, Pte. R.	42
		Kennedy, Pte. J.	42
CHAPTER 10 -		Mathews, S.	42
A New Beginning		McElpatrick, Pte. S.	42
		Mensil	42
		Mound Keep	41
Canaples	37	Peoples, Pte. C.	42
Dale, Pte. J.	38	Redan	41
Evans, Pte. J.	39	Smith, Pte. W.	42
Forceville	39	Stratton, Pte. W.	42
Gordon, Lt. H.C.	37	Thiepval Wood	42
Gordon, Pte. J.	38		
Halloy	37		
Mailly Mailett	39	**CHAPTER 12 -**	
Quigley, Pte. James	37	**An Unfortunate Accident**	
Royal Irish Fusiliers	39		
St. Johnston	37	Adams, J.	54
The Derrys	39	Armstrong, Pte. J.	52
Trimble, W.	38	Authvile	54
Williams, Pte. W.	39	Balleighan	52

Blake, CSM	52	Flackes, W. D.	56
Briggs, Pte.	52	Flackes, Wm.	56
Clarke, Pte. W.	52	Hedauville	55
Derby, Pte. R.	52	Hessey, Lt. Col.	55, 56
Doherty, Pte.	52	L.O.L. 1927	56
Donegal	52, 54	Lord Leitrim	55
Eades, Pte.	52	Martinsart	55
Fleming, Pte.	52	McClintock, Wm. T.	56
Gallaugher, Lt. Henry	52, 53	Roll Book	56
Gillan, Pte. J.	52	Sewell, Capt. W.T.	56
Glasgow	52	Varennes	55
Hall, 2nd Lt. P.	54		
Hessey, Lt. Col.	52		
Hickman, Brig. T.	52	**CHAPTER 14 -**	
Lord Leitrim	52	**Tunnelling, Digging and Shelling**	
Manorcunningham	52		
Martinsart Wood	54	Baizieux	58
McClure, Sgt. J.	54	Ballyshannon	58
McConnell, Pte. R.	52	Brush, Maj. C.H.	58
McCrea, Pte.	52	Carruthers, Pte. H.	60
McFarren, Pte. M.	52	Clairfaye Farm	58
McGowan, Pte. J.	54	Cochrane, J.	60
McIlroy, Pte. H.	52	Eades, Pte. R.	60
McKelvie, Pte. J.	54	Forceville	60, 61
McLaughlin, Pte. D.	52	French Artillery	58
Melanophy, Pte.	52	Gordon Castle	61, 62
Mensil	52	Hessey, Lt. Col.	58
Middlemas, L/Cpl.	52	Hutchinson, Cpl. C.	60
Mumford, Pte. C.	54	Martinsart	61
Newtownbutler	52	McDonald, Pte. R.	60
Royal Irish Rifles	52	McIlroy, Pte. H.	61
Sewell, Capt. W.T.	52	McMaster, Pte. J.	61
St. Johnston	54	Murray, Pte.	60
Stonebridge	52	Myles, Capt. Sproule	58, 60
Will Bridge	54	Nugent, Maj-Gen O.S.	62
		Richardson, L. Cpl. W.	61
		Simpson, Pte. J.	61
CHAPTER 13 -		Spence, Rev. A.	60
Dummy Trenches		Spiers, Pte. W.	60
		Stewart, Pte. J.	61
Dinsmore, Robert	56	Thiepval Wood	58, 60, 61, 63

Wallace, Joe	60	Gunning, Lt. Frank	65
White, Pte. J.	61	Hanna, 2nd Lt.	70
Willis, Sgt. T.	61	Hedauville	70, 73
Wilson, Pte.	60	Herissart	73
		Hewitt, W.E.	74
		Hunter, Pte.	67, 68, 70
CHAPTER 15 -		Irvine, Lt. G.M.	70
The Somme		Jackson, 2nd Lt.	67
		Johnston, 2nd Lt. J.A.	74
Balleighan	65	Kee, L/Cpl. F.	70
Beatty, Sgt.	70	Knight, Lt.	68
Bell, 2nd Lt. A.G.F.	74	Knott DSO, Capt J.E.	74
Bell, Lesley	71	Malseed, 2nd Lt. H.	74
Berguette	73	Manorcunningham	65
Bleakley, R.S.M.	67, 68	McComb, Lt. C.H.	74
Bois De Ploegsteert	74	McCorkell, Lt.	70
Bollezeele	74	McDougal, Cpl.	70
Bowen, T.H.	74	Megaghy, Pte.	69
Browne, Pte.	69	Messines	74
Bruce, George	68	Moore, Capt.	67, 68, 70
Brush, Lt. Col.	66, 70	Moulle	74
Buchanan, Stewart	71	Mountray, Capt. F.C.	74
Bullock, C.S.M.	65	Mulholland, Capt.	67
Burt	71	Nugent, General	73
Conteville	73	O'Brien, J.F.	74
Cooper, L/Cpl.	69	Peacock, Major	67
County Donegal	65, 67, 71	Picken, Capt.	70
Crosbie, Capt. D.E.	68, 69, 70	Porterfield, L/Cpl.	66
Curley, 2nd Lt. J.	74	Quelmes	74
Derrygonnelly	68	Red Lodge	74
Douve	74	Robb, Pte.	69
Elgin Avenue	68, 69	Robertson, J.	74
Elliott, Pte.	69	Romarin	74
Fawkes, C.W.	74	Setques	74
Fenwick, Pte.	69	Sewell, Capt. W.T.	65
Fermanagh	67, 71	Shuter, Brigadier-General	73
Fieuviller	73	Smith, Pte.	70
Firth, Lt. J.	69	Thiepval	64, 70, 71, 72
Gallaugher, Lt. Henry	65, 66, 67, 70	Toland, Pte.	66, 69
Gavin, Lieut.	69	Wallace, Joe	71
Gordon, Lt.	67, 68	Warren, Cpl.	70

Watler	74	Aircraft Farm	82
Wilkinson, E.	74	Bailleul	82, 83
Wilson, Pte.	69	Bleakley, R.S.M.	82
		Bullock C.S.M.	79

CHAPTER 16 -
Distinguished Service

		Clarke, Pte. J.T.	83
		Derry Camp	83
		Dodwell	82
Ballinamallard	78	Donaldson, L/Cpl.	81
Bell, A. G.	76	Donegals	79
Brush, Lt Col	76	Dranoutre	79
Colebrooke	76	Enniskillen Nationalist Volunteers	80
Craven, P.	76	Falls, Major C. F.	82
Crosbie, Capt	76	Fern, L/Cpl.	81, 82
Distinguished Conduct Medal	77, 78	Gas cylinders	81
Distinguished Service Order	76	Halliday, Bro.	82
Doherty, J.	76	Hallowe'en	83
Fleming, W. J.	76	Hunter, J.	82
Forde, G. M.	76	Irish Brigade	80
Gallaugher, H.	76, 77	Knight, Lt.	82
Hanover L.O.L. 215	76	Knobkerries	80, 81
Hunter, J. A.	77	Lewis, Bro.	82
Knott, Capt	76	Marriott, Pte. G.	83
Marne	77	McConnell, J.	82
McCorkell, B. F.	76	McKay, L/Cpl. Alex	81
McKay, L/Cpl	76	Megaghey, L/Cpl. R.	79
Moore, Capt	76, 78	Muir, Lt. A. H.	79
Moutray, F. C.	76	Murphy, Lt. W. A.	79
Pleogsteert Wood	76	O'Hara, Sgt.	81, 82
Pratt, A. C.	78	Orange Lodge	82
Romarin	76, 78	Orgill, Pte.	81, 82
Sherwood Foresters	76	Pleogsteert Wood	79
Tattykeeran	76	Pratt, Major	80
The King	76	Romarin	79
Thompson, J.	78	Scott, Lt. J.	79
Woods, John	78	Sherwood Foresters	79
Wylie, Sgt	77	Stirling Castle	79
		Sweeney, 2nd Lt. T. C.	79

CHAPTER 17 -
Knobkerries by Moonlight

		Taughboyne	81
		The Inniskillings True Blues	82
		Tyrones	79
Adams, 2Lt. T.	80, 82	Wray, L. Cpl. Charles	81

CHAPTER 18 -
At the Moon's Rise

104 Saxon Regiment	86
Ammonal Tube	84, 85, 87
Ballylawn, Co. Donegal	89
Barnhill, Cpl. David	89
Bleakley, R.S.M.	88, 89
Bowes, J.	88
Box Barrage	84, 87
Chaplain	89
Christmas Day 1916	89
Communion Set	89
Enniskillen	84, 88
German hand grenades	84
Haig, Sir Douglas	89
Halesowen	88
Half Way House	89
Hyde Park Corner	89
Johnstone, 2nd. Lt.	84, 86
Kortepyp	89
Malseed, 2nd. Lt.	84
McCartney, H.	89
Military Cross	87
No Man's Land	84
Operation's Order	84
Ploegsteert	89
Pratt Lt. Col.	84
Regimental Museum	89
Rev. Spence	89
Roulston, Robert	87
Sappers	84
Strong, 2nd. Lt.	84, 85, 87, 89
Talbot 2nd. Lt.	84
Walker, John	84

CHAPTER 19 -
Another Year

C.S.M. Lewis, W.	93
Christmas	90
Cpl. Donaldson, T.	93
Cpl. Edwards, J. R.	92
Cpl. Irvine, R.	92
Cpl. Keys, W. R.	92
Cpl. Noble	92
Crosbie, Capt. R.A.M.C.	90
Hazelbrouck	93
Holmes, G.	92
Kemmel Hill	93
Kemmel	93
L/Cpl. Armstrong	93
L/Cpl. Cairns, T.	93
L/Cpl. Hawkesworth, 14 sec.	93
L/Cpl. McGahey, R.	93
L/Cpl. Scott, H.	93
Mann, R.	93
Myles, Capt.	90
Pratt, Lt. Col.	90, 91, 92
Pte. Armstrong, F. S.	93
Pte. Beattie, G. R.	93
Pte. Booth, M.	93
Pte. Burke, J.	93
Pte. Cadden, T.	92
Pte. Cathcart, J.	93
Pte. Clarke, F.	93
Pte. Crozier, F. G.	93
Pte. Dillon	92
Pte. Ditty, J. 13 sec.	93
Pte. Drycott	93
Pte. Evens, J.	92
Pte. Ferris, W.	93
Pte. Foster, W.	93
Pte. Galtraith, J. 16 sec.	93
Pte. Gardiner, W.	93
Pte. Graham, J.	93
Pte. Hollahan, J.	93
Pte. Humphrey, H.	92
Pte. Irvine, W.	93
Pte. Kichiney	93
Pte. Leonard, J.	93

Pte. Little, G.	93	Inniskilling Wood	100
Pte. Lowery, G.	93	Inniskillings	100, 103
Pte. McDonagh, C.	93	Kemmel	96
Pte. McGarrity, R.	93	Knight, Capt. William	98-100, 104
Pte. McGrath	93	Laird, C.S.M.	100
Pte. McIlfatrick	93	Letterkenny	94
Pte. Moore, T.	93	M.M.	105
Pte. Murphy, J.	93	Manorcunningham	94, 102, 103
Pte. Noble, J.	92	Messines	94, 96-101
Pte. Prince, C.	93	Model School	94
Pte. Ryan	93	Moffats Private Academy	94
Pte. Saunders, G.	92	Oosttaverne	100
Pte. Scott	93	Peckham	98
Pte. Simpson	93	Ploegsteert	97
Pte. Stirrip, J. H.	92	Plugstreet Wood	96
Pte. Teirnan, M.	92	Plumer, General Sir Hubert	96
Pte. Thompson, J.	93	Pratt D.S.O.	96, 97, 101, 102
Pte. Thompson, P.	93	Presbyterian	94
Pte. Tipping, J.	93	Spanbroek	94, 101
R.Q.M.S. Brock, W. J.	92	Spanbroekmolen	98
Richards, J.	93	Strazeele	100
Sergt. Armstrong, R.	92	Tempo	94
Sergt. Brabrooke, M.	92	Toland, S.	94
Sergt. Bruce, G. H.	92	Unnamed Wood	100
Sergt. Riley, R.	92	V.C.	101
Sgt. White, H.	93	Wakefield	96, 100
Spanbroek	93	Watson, Rev. A.	103
Trimble, Mr W.	92	Whiting, C.W.	96
Ulster Division Certificate	93	Wyteschaete	98, 99, 102
		Ypres	98
		Zillebeke	97

CHAPTER 20 - Battle of Messines

British	99	**CHAPTER 21 -**	
Canadian Tunnelling Coy	100	**Passchendaele - Fighting in the**	
Flanders	96, 97	**Mud**	
Fluke, Capt. S.	98, 104		
Follit, Lt. W.	96	Admiral	110
Forde, Capt. G.M.	98, 104	Alquines	107
Gallaugher D.S.O. Capt. Henry		Armitage	110
94, 98, 99, 101-104		Arras	109

Bapaume	113	Saint Jean	110
Barastre	113	Schuler Farm	111
Beatty, Pte. J.R.	109	Sprig	107
Bleakley, M.C. R.S.M.	108	Steenbeck	113
Brock, R.Q.M.S.	113	Vlamertinghe	110, 113
Caserne	112	Wieltje	110, 111
Concheviel, Mademoiselle	108	Winnizeele	113
Crosbie, Capt. D.E.	107, 108, 109	Wright, Rev. J.J.	108
Davis Hamilton	107	Ypres	109, 113
Derrygonnelly	107		
Durham	110		
Falls, Capt. C.B.	110	**CHAPTER 22 -**	
Forde, Capt. G.M.	109	**Refitting and Training**	
Fort Hill	111, 112		
French	110	Abraham, 2nd. Lt. R.	117
Gardiner, Sgt. W.	109	Baker, 2nd. Lt. W.	116
Gheluvelt	111	Bertincourt	116
Gough, Sir Hubert	109	Buckley, 2nd. Lt. H.	116
Greaves, C.S.M. J.	109	Donnel, Pte. S.	116
Hamilton, 2nd. Lt. John	108	Elliott, Cpt. W.	116
Hamilton, Margaret	108	Ferguson, Pte. W.	116
Heights	109	Gray, 2nd. Lt. J.	117
Hoozle	107	Hermies	116
Irvine, Capt.	111, 112	Hughes, 2nd. Lt. A.	117
Knight, Capt. W.M.	109	Irvine, Capt. G.M.F.	116
Knott, D.S.O. Major D.E.	111	Johnston, S.	116
Langemarck	111, 113	Legg. 2nd. Lt. H.	116
Langlet	108	Lord Letrim	117
Manorhamilton	108, 112	Milne, 2nd. Lt. G.	116
McComb, Lt.	111	Orgill, Pte. F.	116
McGhee, Pte. P.	109	Robinson, 2nd. Lt. J.M.	116
Messines	109, 110	Spence, Rev. A.	116
Myles, Capt. S.	107	Stett, Cpl. J.	116
Nugent, Gen.	113	Sweeny, 2nd. Lt. T.C.	116
Parke, Sgt. J.	109	Warren, Sgt.	116
Plumer, General	109	Whitlas, Major	116
Pond Farm	112		
Pratt, D.S.O. Lt. Col.	111		
Roger	108	**Chapter 23 - Cambrai**	
Royal Scots	113		
Rutledge, L/Cpl. Willie	108, 112	9th Inniskillings	120

36th Division	119	11th R. Inniskilling Fusiliers	122-124
62nd Division	120	36th (Ulster) Division	124
Achiet-la-Petit	121	109th Inf. Brigade	124
Bapaume	119, 120	Armstrong, Sgt. R.	123
Barrowman, 2nd. Lt. R. S.	120	Bell, Lt. D. J.	123
Battle of Cambrai	119	Bertincourt	122
Bertincourt	121	Charlton M.C., Lt. J. W.	123
Cambrai	120	Comforts Fund	123
Canal du Nord	119	Divisional Follies	123
Carlow	121	Donegals	122
Charlton M.C., Lt. J. W.	121	Eames, L/Cpl. W.	123
County Donegal	120	Edwards, Sgt. J. R.	123
Dewicourt	119	Fawkes, Cpl.	123
Doignies	121	Godfrey, Pte. A. C.	123
Donegal County Council	120	Gregory, L/Cpl.	123
Finney, 2nd Lt.	120	Havrincourt Wood	122
Flesquieres	119	Hessey, Brig. Gen. W. G.	124
Graincourt	119	Hindenburg	122
Havrincourt Wood	118	Law, Pte. H.	123
Hermies	121	Lucheux	123
Hindenburg Line	118	Mertz	122
Infantry	118	Military Medal	123
Inniskilling Brigade	119	Mrs. Hessey	123
Knight, Capt.	119	Neill, Pte. R.	123
Lewis gun	119	Sorel-le-Grand	122
Lifford	120	Tiesseman, Pte. J.	123
Messines	121	Tulip, Pte. O.	123
Moeuvres	121	Tyrones	122
Spoil Heap	120	Welsh Ridge	122
Tyrones	119, 120		
Ulster Volunteers	120		
Velu Wood	118, 119	**CHAPTER 25 -**	
Wagentreiber, Capt. W. H.	120	**The System Still Works**	
Wallace, Joe	118		
		10th Inniskillings	125
		28th Regiment	125
CHAPTER 24 -		Artemps	126
The Unkept Promise		Battle of Cambrai	125
		Battle of St. Quentin	125
9 Inniskillings	122, 123	British Army	125
10th R.I.R.	122	Cairns, Sgt. T.	125

Donegals	126	**CHAPTER 27 -**	
Drumsillagh	125	**And when the War is Over**	
Essingy Station	125		
Hughes, Pte. J.	125	9th Lancers	134, 135
Impartial Reporter	126	36th Ulster Division	131
Jeanne d'Arc	125, 126	Adjutant	130
L.O.L. 347	125	Alexander M.C., Major C.A.M.	134
Letterbreen	125	Archdale M.P., Mr. E.	138
Military Medal	125	Ardagh	133
Nesbitt, Sgt. A.	125	Archdeacon M'Manaway	136, 138
Soleate	125	Ballyshannon	130, 132, 138
St. Simon	125	Bates, Sgt I.	134
Sweeny, Pte. J.	125	Boyhill	131
Tyrones	126	Brigadier-General A. St. Q. Ricardo,	
Ulster Volunteer Force	125	C.M.G., C.B.E., D.S.O.	134-136, 138
		Bullock M.C., Mr. S.	138
		Cambrai	135, 137
		Canon Clements	139
CHAPTER 26 -		Capt. Curley M.C.	138
Farewell to the Eleventh		Carnone	133
		Charlton M.C., Capt. James W.	131
9th Inniskillings	127, 128, 129	Chicele Chair	132
14th R.I.R.	128	Clarke, Mr. S. C.	138
23rd Entrenching Battalion	128	Cleenish Island	133
36th Division	127	Colebrooke River	131
109th Brigade	127, 128	Colour	134-136
Artemps	127	Colour Party	135, 138
Bleakley, M.C. Guy	128	Counties Donegal and Fermanagh	135
Cugny	127	Dail Eirean	132
Curley, Capt.	128	Dann, D.S.O., Lt.-Col. W.R.H.	138
Donegals	128	Davy Donaldson	132
Fermanagh	128	Derrygonnelly	132
Finner	128	Donegal	131, 132, 133
Forde, Lt. Col.	129	Donegal County Council	132
General Hessey	128	Donegal Regiment	138, 139
Grand Seracourt	127	Egypt	132
Noble, Pte. Joseph	128	Enniskillen Garrison	138
Randalstown	128	Enniskillen Model School	131
St. Quentin	128	Falls, Capt. Cyril	131, 132, 134, 138
Tyrones	127	Fermanagh	131
Villnselve	127	Foyle College	132

Gordon M.C., Capt. H. C.	138	New Zealand	130
Hazlett D.C.M., L/Cpl. Louis	130	Newtowncunningham	131
Hessey D.S.O., General W.F.	135-137	Old Comrades Association	138
Hindenburg	130, 137	Omagh	130, 134
Home Guard	130, 131	Oxford	132
Inis Samer	132	Palestine	132
Killykeeran Cross	131	Parish Church	135
King's Colour	134, 136, 137	Passchendaele	137
Knight, Capt. W.M.	135	Portora Royal School	131
Lieut.-Col. J. E. Knott, C.M.G., D.S.O.,	135, 136, 138	Queen's University	131
		Roulston, Robert	131
Lisbellaw	131	Somme	130, 131, 132, 135
Lisburn	132	South Donegal	138
Lough Erne	133	Stephenson, Pte. John	133
Lough Erne cot	133	St. McCartin's Cathedral	
M.M.	130		131, 138, 139
Macedonia	132	The Sprig	134
Main Barracks	134	The Times	132
Martin M.C., Lieut. F. W.	134	Thiepval Glory	133
Masonic	132	Thiepval House	133
Maxwell, Mr. Bill	138	Tiernan, Matt	133
Maxwell, Mr. W. J. R.	138	Trimble, Mr. Copeland	138
McFarland M.M., Mr. J. J.	138	U.V.F.	137, 138
McIlfatrick, A.	133	Ulster Special Constabulary	134
McMullen M.M., Mr. A.	138	W. Clendinning M.M.	138
McMullen, L/Cpl. Alex	130	Wallace, Cpl. Joe	130
Messine	137	Waterloo	132
Myles M.C., Major Sproule	132	Wyteschaete	135, 137
Myles, Robert	132	Ypres	130, 135, 137

Thanks

This book could not have been written without the help and co-operation of a considerable number of people. I am very grateful for the kindness and hospitality shown to me by those whom I came in contact with in the course of my research. I was very encouraged by the interest and willing assistance shown to me.

I can not mention everyone individually but I am deeply indebted to the following:

Major George Stephens M.B.E. D.L. Curator of The Royal Inniskilling Fusiliers Regimental Museum. In making all the Regimental Archives available, for his cheerful patience and unfailing courtesy, this was a pleasant task. Margaret Mulligan and Dick Thompson, staff of the Regimental Museum for their assistance.

Joanna McVey for the use of the Impartial Reporter archives.

Miss Eileen Gallaugher and Miss Jean Gallaugher for copies of all the letters of their uncle Capt. Henry Gallaugher D.S.O. and permission to publish some of them.

Mr. & Mrs. Ivan Noble, Cloghbally for proof reading and valuable information.

Major M. Dickie for photo of Lord Leitrim.

Mr. J. Buchanan, Mr. R. Roulston and Mr. T. Hamilton for photographs.

Mr. Gardiner Mitchell for advice and reproduction of some of the photographs.

Mrs. Eva Hassard, Monea.
Mr. W. Parkes, Derrygonnelly.
Miss Jean Bleakley and Mr. Jim Bleakley, Enniskillen.
Mrs. R. Vaughan, Antrim.
Mr. T. Canning M.A. Dip. Ed., Armagh.
Mr. W. F. A. Charlton, Bangor.
Mr. A. Roberts, Londonderry.
Mrs. E. James, Christchurch, New Zealand.
Mr. C. King, Ballyshannon.

Mrs. Lynn Buick N.E.E.L.B., Ballymena.
Corinna Power of The Impartial Reporter for artwork and indexing.
Staff of W.E.E.L.B. Enniskillen.
Mr. Sean Murphy B.A., B.E.M., Waterford.
Yvonne Maxwell for all her patience and skill with the word-processing.
Mr. T. McBride, Linenhall Library, Belfast.
L.O.L. 1927 for use of copy of Minute Book.
Mr. Ian Bartlett, Londonderry.
Mr. E. Sullivan, Waterford.
The Somme Association.
Rev. N.E. Dorrans B.Sc., Ray Presbyterian Church.
Mr. D. Canning, Newbuildings, Londonderry.
Mr. & Mrs. R. McCausland, Londonderry.
The late Mr. Bill Maxwell.
Mr. N. McIlfatrick, Lisbellaw.

My wife Nancy for all her help and thoroughness in research and for her encouragement and patience.

Acknowledgments

Fermanagh District Council.

The Blackstaff Press for kind permission to quote a short extract from "The Road To The Somme" by Philip Orr.

The Imperial War Museum for the use of photographs.